# Hey There, DUMPLING!

## 100 RECIPES for Dumplings, Buns, Noodles, and Other Asian Treats

By Kenny Lao and Genevieve Ko
Photographs by Lucy Schaeffer

# INTRODUCTION

One night, I was at this super-buzzy, New York-y party and a friend introduced me as "Kenny, the founder and owner of Rickshaw Dumplings" to a group of polished, suited lawyers and finance types. One of the women screamed, "Oh my god! I love your Thai chicken dumplings!" loud enough for the whole room to hear. A second later, a guy yelled from across the floor, "Peking duck dumplings rule!" And the rest of the night, people kept coming up to me to tell me their favorites: vegan edamame, Korean beef bulgogi, sweet potato. At first I thought, "Whoa. This is crazy." Then I thought, "Man! This is awesome!" Growing up in Pasadena, California, as the kind of kid who was regularly sent to the principal's office, I never thought that one day I'd be recognized because of dumplings in New York City. But that's the power of dumplings. It's what's inside that counts.

I spent a decade running that dumpling company, and there's one thing I can say with absolute certainty: Everyone loves dumplings! What food lovers across the country don't know yet is how easy dumplings are to make at home. And how fun they are to make with friends. That's where this book comes in.

Dumpling-making parties totally rule. They were the ultimate inspiration behind my business and the reason I still love making dumplings at home today. There's a great shared experience in wrapping and cooking dumplings with friends and family—it's a little competitive, a lot of yummy.

Doing dumplings is a kind of casual, social get-together where you end up with chopsticks clashing across the table for hot "yeah-we-just-made-this!" food. In these pages, you'll find awesome recipes for noodles, salads, soups, side dishes, snacks, drinks, and desserts; cool cooking and party tips; and memories from my Chinese-American upbringing.

**Party On**

I lived for dumpling parties as a kid; they made me feel like I was part of a way bigger family. When I was three, my parents divorced. So it was just me and my mom in Pasadena, living near the curvy, hilly streets by the Rose Bowl, where every other house has a big USC football flag hanging over the front door. My mom and I are really close, so our peaceful lives together had this great feeling of us against the world. But growing up as an only child with just my mom, I always wondered what I was missing out on. I wondered if every night was like dumpling night...

On dumpling nights, which rolled around every few weeks, the Tan family would come over for dinner. The Tans lived down the street and had a daughter, Tracy, who was a year older than me, and a son, Jason, a year younger. We aren't related to them, but they are definitely family. As a kid, I'd get so excited about our dumpling nights, I'd wear my favorite red E.T. t-shirt. You know, the one where the fingers are touching? (Whoa, eighties!) My mom would warn me, "Kenny! You'll get your favorite shirt dirty!" She was always right, but it was totally worth it.

I'd wait by the door and swing it open when I saw them walk out of their house. The second they stepped into mine, the whole energy in the room would shift. We'd all get chatty-chatty and the noise would build like the Dolby surround sound ad before movies rolled. I'd get enveloped in that frenetic familial energy and start bouncing off the walls before settling down for dumpling duty.

Everyone always headed straight for the kitchen. There was no formality to our dumpling parties, but there was definitely a system. We worked assembly-line style, setting up the counter with spots for making fillings, stuffing, wrapping, and all the way down to the stove for pan-frying and steaming. On the other side of the stove, we set up a sauce station like a cocktail cart. I had to start at the bottom of the prep totem pole when I was young, the way I did as an adult in high-end kitchens. All I got to do was plop the stuffing in the wrappers. Then I stepped up to wrapping, along with the other kids. Woohoo! From there, I graduated to making fillings and sauces and, finally, to the stove. By the time Jason and I were in high school, we got fry duty and steam duty. We nailed the system and kept the dumplings coming out batch after perfect batch.

That may sound intense, but it was actually totally relaxing. Once you figure out how to make dumplings—and it's way easy—you get into muscle-memory mode. I still get into that mode when I throw dumpling parties with friends. Just like on my childhood nights with the Tans, we gossip and get zen-like comfortable hanging out, all while turning out hundreds of dumplings. Whatever we don't eat that night, we freeze to tide us over until the next party. But that feeling of just chilling and chatting and stuffing our faces with hot dumplings—that's the best. It turns a night with friends into the sort of family night I imagine big families have. I'd never go so far as to call my childhood dumpling nights

"dinner parties" because the casual communal cooking was the point. But they were really special.

Everyone loves dumplings and knows how tasty they are when they get them from a restaurant. But the point of making dumplings at home is to enjoy the process with others. Best party ever—plain and simple. It doesn't hurt that you end up with a freezer full of 10-minute dinners!

## Dumpling Delicious

I've spent my whole life making and eating dumplings, and my all-time faves are in this book. They're packed with flavors everyone loves. And I don't just do dumplings. Even at our childhood parties, we always had salads—we're such Californians!—and noodles, too. Whatever veg didn't make it into a dumpling filling ended up as sides. Of course, a party isn't a party without drinks and desserts. I'm drawing on all the dishes I've learned and loved over the years to show you how outrageously fun and easy it is to throw together a dumpling party. Or a simple dinner on any night, for that matter.

At my family dumpling parties, we covered all the proteins, from pork to beef to turkey to chicken to seafood. We did tons of vegetarian options too, even though none of us was actually a vegetarian. And we stirred those same veggies into the meat fillings. The ones I really loved were dark, leafy greens like baby spinach worked into ground chicken or turkey so you could see the green under the thin wrappers. So gorgeous! My mom loves cilantro, so she'd chop a whole huge bunch for her specialty, cilantro and pork dumplings (page 37).

We all seasoned the fillings with our basic pantry items: soy sauce, sesame oil, rice vinegar, Shaoxing wine, chiles, sugar. We'd use those same staples to make awesome sauces. We all got into mixing different concoctions. That's how I learned early on the basics of balancing sweet, sour, salty, and spicy by tasting and experimenting. That's the great thing about dumplings: The process isn't complicated. Just build a basic pantry of supermarket ingredients, then stuff the dumplings and whip up the dips. In this book, you'll also find a mix-and-match chart to help pair tasty dips with different dumplings (page 114).

When I was nine, my mom remarried and I got an older stepsister. A little while later, I got a baby half-sister. And I got a food-loving stepdad who won me over by taking me along on every single dinner date with my mom when he was courting her. On our first date (well, his first date with mom), he laid out one rule for me: "Kenny, I want to bring you with us everywhere. But don't order off the kids' menu. It's stupid for you to be going around with us and eating only grilled cheese and hot dogs." He didn't have to worry, because I had always been a really good eater who tried and loved everything.

I'll never forget the Saturday morning he took us to Wolfgang Puck's Spago for brunch. We sat out in the Austria-meets-Hollywood fairytale garden, in those fantastic eighties pastel-cushioned patio seats, and I ordered the eggs Benedict. Holy Toledo! They blew my mind! They sat the poached egg on focaccia instead of an English muffin and confettied it with these pickled grilled peppers that were a sharp kick to the runny eggs and creamy hollandaise. Even as a kid, I was struck by how genius that dish was. Those years of dining out were the first time I had an inkling of what I'd end up doing with my life. Seeing food transformed at Spago into

something unexpected but familiar in such a spectacular setting was as awesome to me as getting grilled pastrami Reubens at Barney's, our family hangout set in a block of porn shops. Other nights, we hit Noodle King, our go-to for doughy northern Chinese pork dumplings, veggie buns, and stewed beef soup noodles served with chilled, sharp tofu and garlicky cucumber salads. The grimy little linoleum-tiled restaurant was set in this crumbling art deco building, but it served the best Chinese comfort food. No frills, ultimate satisfaction.

## Stuff-My-Face Study Abroad

I left those happy eating years with my new family of five for Brown University. I arrived as an International Studies major, gunnin' for the best grades and clamoring for the top. My parents never pushed me to do any one thing professionally, but they showed me how to succeed in business by starting their own real estate development company after they got married. I learned a lot in my classes, but it was my year outside of Providence that really changed me. I spent a semester studying abroad in China and basically ate my way through the country.

It wasn't my first time in China; growing up, I had gone there on family trips. My earliest visit was with my mom, right after she divorced my biological dad. Even though I was only four at the time, I still have vivid memories of how awesome breakfast there was: steamed or fried soft, yeasty buns or flaky onion rolls on one side of the plate, steaming rice porridge or soup on the other, spiked with spicy pickles. The contrast between the bitter cold outside and the hot food inside made for the best eating experience ever.

Everybody dumpling!

By the time I went to China on my own at age twenty, I had been a few other times with my family. Each trip, all I did was eat and eat and talk about the food. When I met my study-abroad group, I was surprised that there were students who had priorities other than eating while traveling. Then I met Bridget. We ate our way through China like no one's business. I can't even tell you how much we friggin' ate there. Dumplings and dumplings, then on to other street food stalls, where we'd grab flaky sesame bread sandwiches, soy milk, and eggs fried into crêpes. When we discovered how cheap Peking duck was there, we had it for every meal until our bodies shut down. To recover, we had cleansing *la mien* (hand-pulled) noodles cooked in huge vats of hot broth.

On the other end of the spectrum, I sampled the haute cuisine of the nouveau riche and ex-pats. I was a poor student, but I landed an internship at a consulting firm. Those Chinese businessmen would take me to these crazy places and I kinda had to eat everything. Not that I'm complaining; it was all delicious. I'll never forget this shocking sea urchin dish: It was cooked and hot, but served with an al dente texture and oceany mildness. Not a lot of seasoning, but heaps of flavor. That dish, like so many at these high-end places, showed me how the best Asian food relies on impeccable ingredients as much as Western food does.

That was also true at the hole-in-the-wall dumpling joints. In Beijing, they used garlic that was so fresh, it was juicy when raw. There was a whole art form to peeling those pungent cloves to stuff into chewy thick wrappers with sesame oil, or to steeping them in black vinegar for dipping sauce. That unusual combo of clean flavors was fantastic. Other vegetarian varieties used greens that were so fresh, you could really taste their anisey sweetness or their crunchy celery-like savoriness. I loved the large variety of mushrooms—some earthy, some funky, some mellow.

As I traveled south, I found that the dumpling wrappers got thinner and the fillings more flavorful, and I preferred them that way. The handmade dough in Beijing meant that the dumplings were more of a starch, a necessarily hearty dish for the harsh winters. The delicate southern-style dumpling skins meant the end products had to be smaller —which meant I could eat more of them! But the other distinction was that the dumplings themselves were less dependent on the accompanying sauces for flavor. In Szechuan especially, the insides had to be powerful enough to counter the chili oil that went on top.

My nonstop eating tour of Chinese dumplings was like a never-ending version of my dumpling parties at home. I missed cooking with my family, but I gained a new shared experience with Bridget, who became like a sister to me, and, in a weird larger sense, with the millions of Chinese dumpling eaters all around me. I returned home with strong food memories, a renewed love of dumplings, and no clue about what to do after graduation.

## Going Pro

As a kid, the closest I ever got to nailing my future career was during a speech contest in eighth grade. I said I was going to be an entrepreneur. My parents had just quit their secure full-time jobs and bought a house as their first real estate development project. We moved in, renovated it, and moved on (actually, in) to the next project. I got really involved in their business, doing the logo for the company, tagging along to collect rents, wrapping quarters for the laundry machines. I knew I'd want my own business someday, but I had no idea it was going to be food and restaurants, and I didn't know how it was going to happen.

My first year right out of college, I became an analyst at an economic consulting firm in Boston. At the end of my first year, my bosses told me I was doing great and handed over a fat bonus. Looking at the amount, I asked, "Is this the maximum I can get?" They smiled and quickly replied, "Yes! That's the highest amount for first-year analysts." I took the money and quit. I got pulled into that office culture in the first place; I never wanted to be there. It was just what Ivy grads did and it was a lot of money, but I wasn't satisfied. I spent most of that year sorting out what I really wanted to do in my head. I knew I loved restaurants. I kinda took a leap of faith and decided to try that world.

I started doing my homework, researching which restaurant groups were growing fast, and Drew Nieporent's name kept popping up. I did my own business analysis of their group to determine what they needed for successful growth to scale their business. I wrote a proposal for how to implement a rigorous development program for

managers to make each restaurant self-sufficient. I was so young, so naïve!

And I was so determined to get it into Drew's hands somehow. I went old school and looked up his name in the white pages. How many Nieporents could there be? "Sybil Nieporent" sounded promising, so I rang her up. It was his mother. She gave me a number and said, "You call Drew and say that Sybil told you to call." He called me back in five minutes. The power of mothers, right?

I didn't waste any time: "Drew, I'd love to shoot you this business plan for your company." He replied, shocked, "You have a business plan for me? Well, send it to my business partner, Michael Bonadies. He's the one spearheading our growth." Not long after, I ended up meeting with Drew, Michael, and Marty Shapiro—all three partners of Myriad Restaurant Group—in one day. It was a crazy "interview," but it got me a job.

I did everything from running fish from Tribeca Grill to Nobu, photocopying receipts, bussing tables, pouring wine, and working catered events to cooking on the line. I'd start with a breakfast meeting with Michael, take reservations at Nobu, run to do a preshift lunch front of house at Tribeca Grill, then run to do preshift garde manger back of house at Centrico, then prep dinner at Montrachet, then work tables at Nobu.

It was so tiring working those hours, but I loved it when the restaurants got super-duper busy. When I was training to be a server at Tribeca Grill, I remember getting this floating feeling when everyone on staff was in the zone. We instinctively knew which tables needed bread, which ones needed water. We dropped the apps right on time,

You have
such pretty
pleats.

It's what's
inside that
counts.

other side of the table, too. Maybe that explains the weird trajectory my career took. I went from working super high-end restaurants to opening fast-casual joints to operating food trucks. Those years with Drew actually led me down this path and taught me a ton. I developed an amazing palate by tasting a huge range of dishes at restaurant openings, and I put all those tastes and ideas into the recipes in this book, as well as the lessons in pairing real hospitality with food. I'm passing on the skills and experiences I got from professional dining rooms that will make your dumpling gatherings the best dinner parties you ever throw.

## Doing Dumplings

After 9/11, the restaurant business in New York City really dried up. I decided it was a good time for me to go to business school and figure out what I wanted to do next. I knew I wanted to stay in the hospitality industry, but wasn't sure in what capacity.

Figuring that out was a great perk of b-school, but the best thing I got out of it was David Weber, my former business partner. I had been toying with the idea of a dumpling shop for a while, combining my favorite food in the world with my love of the restaurant business. When the entrepreneurship class announced a new business competition, I told David, "I'm actually thinking about doing this. You're gonna help me write this business plan. But if you're gonna write this plan, I need to know if you're in or out." David got really into it and we entered our dumpling restaurant plan. That year, we didn't make it past the first round. The next year, we didn't win either. But we did start looking for investors. I hated asking for money, but it went

and we could all feel it. It's such an amazing, addictive thrum, that vibration in the dining room when it all comes together. Even after I got to do more of the big stuff as special projects director, I loved the high-low nature of my job. It's kinda how I function even today—and how I pull off perfect dumpling parties. You're getting down and dirty with wrapping dumplings to get a really refined, beautiful meal. After all the messy cooking together, you and your friends end up with a big, fantastic party where everyone shares a food-fueled energy.

The best part about dumplings: They're really not fancy food. Early in my career, Drew taught me that high-end cooking isn't the only source of real satisfaction. I guess I already knew that because it's how I like to eat. I've gotten as much pleasure from four-star haute cuisine temples as I have from hole-in-the-wall dumpling joints. Drew helped me see that I can enjoy the same dichotomy on the relatively easily. Because people love dumplings! I ended up being the face of the business and the link to the food. I'm not a chef—I'm a really good home cook—but Anita Lo is a phenomenal chef. And we were lucky enough to snag her for Rickshaw.

To complement the recipes from my Rickshaw days, I've included my personal favorites. These come from combos I did with my mom growing up, with my (vegetarian!) husband now, and with (omnivorous) friends. I use ingredients that can be found in major American supermarkets and techniques that are totally unintimidating. Even though these dumplings are easy to make, they're super-pretty, too. They're pleated and packaged like elegant little purses, and the colorful fillings show through the thin wrappers. As for flavors, I'm not getting too hung up on authenticity. I like to go over

and beyond cultural boundaries to create amazing international food. As long as it makes your mouth happy, it rocks.

The dumplings made from the recipes in this book are going to be better than any you've had at restaurants. Seriously. Because the main technique used—the one I've loved most since I was a kid— is pan-frying. Pan-fried dumplings are brazenly browned on one side and soft and juicy on the other. Yum, right?

You can make great dumplings! I promise. Over the years, I've learned that you can teach anyone to fill, wrap, and cook these babies like a frickin' pro. All you need is to be crazy excited about trying them! So get pumped! Let's do this!

**Ode to Anita**

I couldn't do a dumpling book without including the recipes from Rickshaw, my former dumpling company. Superstar chef Anita Lo created those dishes. I fell in love with her Rickshaw recipes at first taste and still love them every time I make them at home.

Anita is the chef and owner of Annisa in New York City's Greenwich Village. She and her restaurant have won a gazillion awards because her food totally rocks. I've eaten at the best restaurants all over the world and Annisa ranks way up there. When I decided to start a dumpling restaurant, I knew I wanted her to be a part of the team. I contacted Anita during my first year of business school and said, "I'm doing this dumpling concept and I think it'd be great for you." I was pumped! Working with Anita was a dream. I was so happy to have an amazing chef working on this concept, and she came up with an unbelievable menu.

Because they're shaped like the ingots of ancient Chinese currency, dumplings symbolize prosperity and wealth. That's why they're chowed down during Lunar New Year celebrations. Beats eating a dollar bill.

The core of this book's recipes is the original collection of dumplings, dips, sides, and sweets Anita developed for Rickshaw. She has the uncanny ability to be very authentic to Asian flavors, but to make the dishes palatable to all other tastes as well. So she didn't do durian or bitter melon dumplings, but she threw aromatic Thai basil into the chicken dumplings that became Rickshaw's runaway bestseller. Anita nailed the recipes right out of the gate. Her recipes are very ingredient-driven and chef-inspired, but they're also really doable. Somehow, she manages to create complex, well-balanced tastes with easy-to-find ingredients and basic techniques. In short, genius.

Lovers of Rickshaw Dumplings will recognize some of Anita's signature recipes in this book. In addition to the bestselling Chicken & Thai Basil Dumplings (page 63) with Spicy Peanut Dip (page 106), there are a bunch of her recipes in here, from the Classic Pork & Chinese Chive (page 36) to Kimchi Beef (page 60), Szechuan Chicken (page 64), Peking Duck (page 72), Shrimp Nori (page 76), Pea Shoots & Leek (page 79), and Mustard Greens & Mustard Seeds (page 84). And, of course, there are her awesome Chocolate Soup Dumplings (page 190) for dessert! For this book, we streamlined some of her signature sides, like the stuffed buns, noodle soups, and salads, to make them doable for all home cooks. But the essence of the originals is definitely still there.

Even though there are no more Rickshaw restaurants and food trucks, I'm thrilled that I still get to taste Anita's dumplings when I prepare them at home. You will be, too.

TOOLS

**17**
MEASURING
SPOONS

1/4 tsp = 1.25ml
1 tsp
15ml
1/8 tsp = 0.6ml

**16**
MANDOLINE

**8**
BAMBOO
STEAMER

**15**
CHOPSTICKS

WHISK

FISH
SPATULA

**11**

**9**
CHEF'S
KNIFE

WOODEN
DOWEL

**12**

PARING
KNIFE

**10**

**14**
MEASURING
CUPS

**13**

SIEVE **5**

CHINESE
SOUPSPOONS

**6**

**1**

WOK

**5**

**3**
PREP
BOWLS

**2**

NONSTICK
SKILLET

**4**

WOODEN
SPOONS

TONGS **7**

Here's what I keep handy for making dumpling parties supereasy. Of course, I use everything here nearly every night for regular meals, too! You can find all the Asian stuff in well-stocked kitchen supply shops.

**1  Wok**

Go for the real thing—carbon steel. That's what my grandma, mom, and generations of Chinese cooks rely on. Carbon steel woks heat up fast and evenly, last forever, and, best of all, come pretty cheap. So you can splurge on a 14-gauge steel that won't dent and warp every time you bang it around. Don't go totally traditional, though. Round-bottomed woks work only if you have a massive burner that cradles it. For our flat Western stovetops, you want a flat-bottomed wok that then flares out on the sides. I'm partial to the northern-style single-handled woks because I think they're easier to use. The trickiest part of using a carbon steel wok is keeping it seasoned. It doesn't really apply here because we're just steaming dumplings, but if you want to try stir-frying, start by scrubbing your brand-new wok with hot soapy water. After it's totally dry, heat it on the highest setting your burner will go until it smokes. (Turn on the exhaust fan and open the windows!) Carefully turn the pan to heat the whole surface. Oil a paper towel or kitchen towel, grip it with long tongs, and rub the oil all over the superhot surface. Done! After each use, wash it with soapy hot water and a soft sponge. Dry it well and rub it with a little oil.

**2  Nonstick Skillet**

You don't want a nonstick wok, but a nonstick skillet ensures your pan-fried dumplings will flip out beautifully every single time. (If you're a total pro with a well-seasoned cast-iron skillet, use it! Just be sure your muscles are up to flipping it.) Any size works, as long as your burner can heat the whole bottom. You'll need a lid, too. As long as it covers the top, it's good.

**3  Prep Bowls**

A set of cute small- and medium-size bowls works well for creating dumpling party assembly lines. You can also use them for a DIY dipping sauce station.

**4  Wooden Spoons**

My go-to stirring implement is actually my hand. Sometimes, though, a spoon comes in handy, especially if I need to stir hot soup!

**5  Sieve**

A set of fine-mesh strainers gets bitty bits out of mixes that I want smooth. Anytime I'm making a big batch of tea, I prefer to mix whole leaves with the water and just pour it all through a sieve. Also in the same strainer family are mesh colanders. A nice big one is all you need.

**6  Chinese Soupspoons**

You must eat soup dumplings—and soup noodles—out of these flat-bottomed spoons. They're deep enough to hold liquid and solids all in one bite.

**7 Tongs**

Bamboo steamers get hot! To remove them from the wok, I grip the edges with tongs and lift them out. I never use tongs to pick up dumplings though—they can break the skins.

**8 Bamboo Steamer**

Not only do they circulate steam perfectly, they also impart a mouthwatering earthy aroma. Plus, they're pretty enough to go straight from stove to table. Final bonus: They're cheap! Buy a lot!

**9 Chef's Knife**

What can I say? I learned to cook in a French kitchen. If you're a pro with a Chinese cleaver, feel free to use it for all your chopping. I prefer a super sharp chef's knife.

**10 Paring Knife**

This little baby works wonders for slivering ginger and scallions. Plus, it's my go-to tool for checking to see if dumplings or buns are cooked through all the way.

**11 Fish Spatula**

Traditionally used for flipping fish fillets, this thin spatula is also ideal for getting dumplings out of the pan if they stick. It's really flat and flexible and slightly offset, so you can wiggle and slide it under the stubbornly stuck dumplings without ripping their skins.

**12 Whisk**

There's no better tool for making dressings and sauces. I like to use heavy whisks that don't get all bendy and warped over time.

**13 Wooden Dowel**

I've tried rolling dumpling wrappers and bun dough with a regular rolling pin and it's really hard. A little dowel (about 4 inches / 10 cm long) fits perfectly in one hand and easily rolls out little rounds, one at a time.

**14 Measuring Cups**

The Chinese way to cook is to add everything to taste. But I like a little precision sometimes.

**15 Chopsticks**

The most brilliant kitchen tool ever. They're great for eating, but they're the best for cooking, too. They can pick up anything delicately, poke and prod, stir, mix, and even lightly whisk. Be sure to use wooden chopsticks for cooking; plastic ones can't withstand heat. I prefer straight sticks, but ones with tapered tips work well, too.

**16 Mandoline**

Instead of splurging on a fancy French contraption, go for the compact Benriner Japanese mandoline. It has a plastic body, but a super sharp steel slicing blade. Just watch your fingers when you're creating paper-thin slices!

**17 Measuring Spoons**

Of course, they're used for measuring. But I also think they're great for scooping filling into dumplings. Double-duty tools are the best!

# INGREDIENTS

**2** STAR ANISE

**3** CAYENNE PEPPER

**4** SZECHUAN PEPPERCORNS

**5** LIMES

**9** GINGER

**6** TOFU

**8** CILANTRO

**7** GARLIC

It's amazing to me how you can basically get anything in big supermarkets nowadays. That makes dumplings really easy to pull together. Extra-esoteric ingredients are described in the recipes they go with. This is just my list of essentials for basic dumplings or any tasty Asian cooking.

**1 Dumpling Wrappers (not pictured)**

As described on page 22, I use flour wrappers that don't have any egg in them. I prefer the Twin Marquis brand that you can find in Asian markets, but I've also tried a bunch of other brands. They all work, but vary in thickness, chew, and taste. You can experiment with whatever you find and choose your favorite. Wrappers keep in the fridge for only a few days before turning funny, but they can be frozen, still wrapped, for up to three months. Thaw them fully in the fridge overnight before using.

**2 Star Anise**

Look for fresh whole ones that hit you with a scent of warm anise. This cool-looking spice is native to China and related to aniseed. It's the source of that elusive scent you sometimes get in Chinese sauces.

**3 Cayenne Pepper**

Cayenne is the best source of straight-up heat. There are some tasty freshly ground chile powders in Chinese markets that you can try, but if you don't want to trek out for those, stick to this staple for adding a hit of heat.

**4 Szechuan Peppercorns**

These are from Szechuan, but they're not really peppercorns. They're the husks of the prickly ash bush and belong in the citrus family. That's why they were banned from the United States for years; they potentially carried a virus that could destroy citrus crops. They've gotten the all-clear from the USDA and now can be found in specialty stores and spice markets. The most amazing thing about these is their numbing effect. They're not actually spicy the way chiles are, but they leave a tingling sensation on your lips and tongue that accentuate heat when they're paired with chiles.

**5 Limes**

Most people stash lemons; I keep limes. Their acidity is ideal for Asian food and, of course, cocktails and drinks.

**6 Tofu**

I love tofu in all its forms—silken soft to firm and dry. The national brands available in supermarkets work well. Just be sure to buy the unflavored varieties. If you ever make it to a Chinese market and see fresh tofu, give it a try. It'll be a revelation.

**7 Garlic**

Whenever possible, buy fat, fresh cloves. You should be able to smell it through the paper-thin skin and when you give it a squeeze, it should feel nice and firm.

**8 Cilantro**

My mom's favorite herb defines much of Asian cuisine. Go for organic here (and everywhere!) because you want to use the stems and roots. There's a lot of flavor there, and you want to be sure to chop it all up for your dumplings and other dishes.

**9 Ginger**

Fresh hands of ginger have smooth, shiny skin that's taut. Old ginger is all wrinkly and sad. Obviously, look for the fresh stuff. When the skin is thin, I keep it on and just scrub it well before chopping.

**10 Scallions**

Long green onions, also known as scallions, are the allium that define much of Chinese cooking. Be sure to get fresh, perky stalks!

**11 Rice Vinegar**

I love a bit of sour in my sauces and dressings. This variety has a subtle acidity and even a teeny bit of sweetness. The Marukan brand is the most readily available and works just fine.

**12 Soy Sauce**

There are countless varieties of this pantry staple. Whole aisles of Asian markets are devoted to this one condiment. Artisan producers mix up small batches around the country now, too. If you don't want to splurge on a fancy brand and don't have access to a good Asian market, Kikkoman works well. For those who need to watch their sodium intake, you can use the lower-sodium option.

**13 Sesame Oil**

A little goes a long way with roasted sesame oil. Buy a little bottle because the oil can go rancid over time. Keep it in a cool, dark place and sniff before using to make sure it's still fresh.

**14 Mint**

Fresh! I love fresh! Vietnamese mint tastes especially good with Asian cuisine, but plain old spearmint works fine. Don't use peppermint though, unless you're making desserts or want a taste of Christmas. It contains menthol, which makes it too assertive for my savory dishes.

**15 Napa Cabbage**

Every market carries this cabbage. It's a cornerstone of dumplings: The chopped leaves lighten dense meat fillings and the soft edges are ideal for lining bamboo steamers.

**16 Snow Peas**

I use these in dumplings, but also enjoy them as a snack!

**17 Shiso Leaves**

Also known as perilla, this Japanese herb tastes like a cross between basil and mint and has a slightly fuzzy texture. There's even a citrus note in this subtle herb. I love using it as a gorgeous garnish, too.

**18 Pea Shoots**

Come spring, farmers' markets sell superfresh pea shoots. I use them in dumpling fillings, as a garnish, and even for quick stir-fries.

**19 Coconut Milk**

Coconut milk is the result of grating coconut meat. When you eat Southeast Asian cuisines, this is often the creamy base for curries and sauces. It is silky, rich, and way tasty.

# DUMPLINGS 101

You ready? Making dumplings is super easy. Just ask P. Diddy. When I was on Martha Stewart's show, she had him on as a guest during our segment. We even got him to make dumplings! Even if you're not a music-media mogul, you can do it too. Chinese kids start when they're toddlers. I swear. I used to teach adults of all cooking levels how to make dumplings at Brooklyn Kitchen. By the end of our two-hour class, they'd be wrapping like pros and having so much fun. Once you get the hang of it, you can do them in your sleep. The key is to get all set up first.

# THE
# ANATOMY
## OF A
# DUMPLING

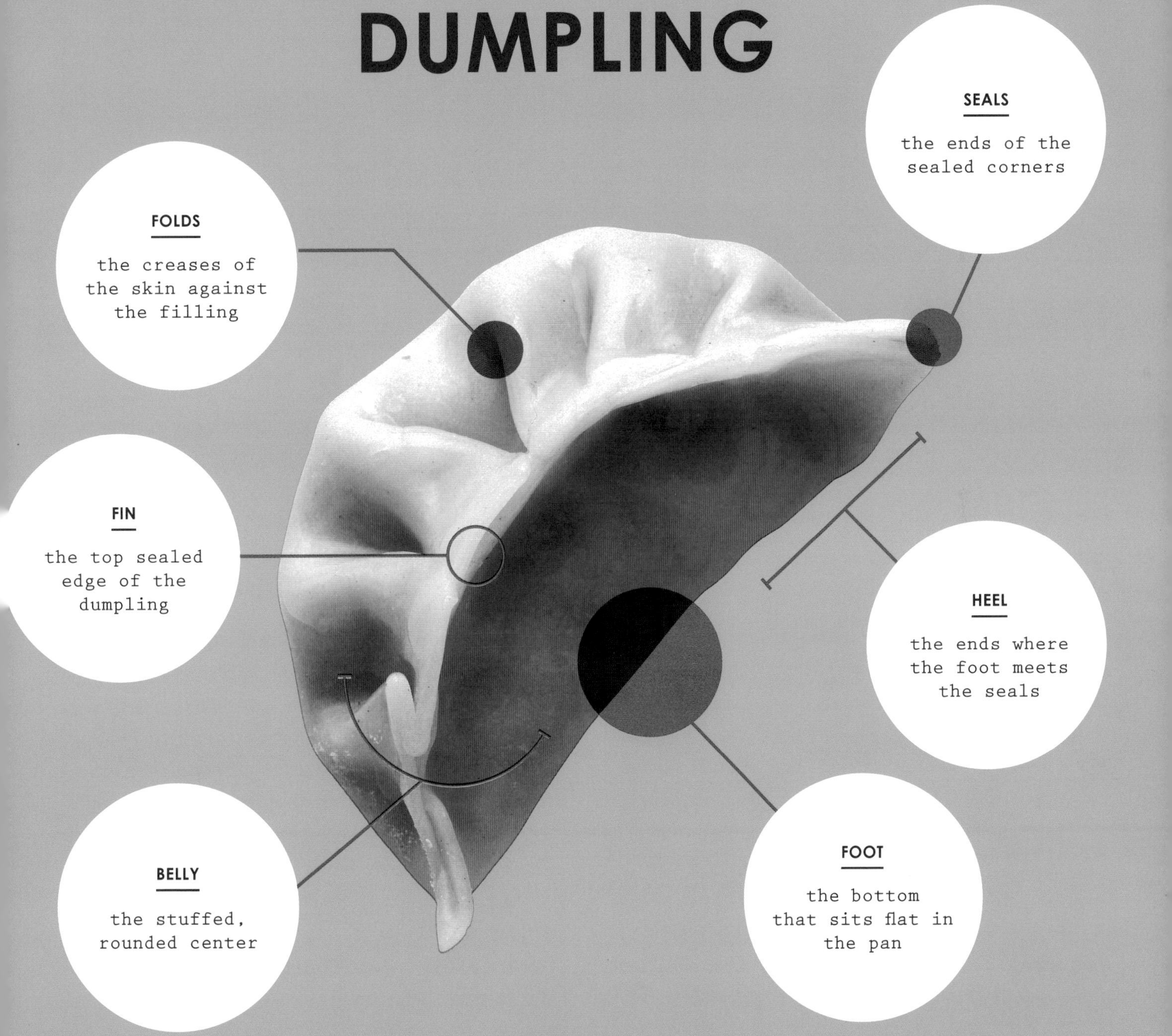

**SEALS**

the ends of the
sealed corners

**FOLDS**

the creases of
the skin against
the filling

**FIN**

the top sealed
edge of the
dumpling

**HEEL**

the ends where
the foot meets
the seals

**BELLY**

the stuffed,
rounded center

**FOOT**

the bottom
that sits flat in
the pan

# PREP THE DECK

FOLD TOWARD THE CENTER

PORK & SHRIMP DUMPLINGS (PAGE 41)

1. Get a foot or so of a work surface nice and clean. Your kitchen counter works fine. A big cutting board does too.

2. Have a flat plate or rimmed pan lined with waxed paper or parchment paper ready. This is where you're going to put your finished dumplings. If you're planning on freezing the dumplings right away (see page 42), use a rimmed pan, but be sure to use one that fits in your freezer. (I've totally zonked on that before and used a pan bigger than my freezer.)

3. You need a pack of round flour dumpling wrappers, sometimes labeled potsticker or gyoza wrappers. You can buy them in regular supermarkets nowadays. If you can't find them there, they'll definitely be at your nearest Asian grocery. They should be 4 to 5 inches (10 to 12 cm) in diameter, thin enough to flap around, and whitish. (The yellow ones are for wontons and have egg in the dough; don't use those.) Each pack should have 40 to 50 wrappers, the number you'll need for my filling recipes. (I especially like the Twin Marquis brand, but have also used TMI Shanghai-Style wrappers with success.)

GOTTA
KEEP 'EM
MOIST

KEEP IT
SIMPLE:
WATER
WORKS!

INVITE
YOUR FRIENDS!
MORE HANDS
=
MORE
DUMPLINGS!

Wrappers are easiest to fold and seal when they're at room temperature, so take them out of the fridge first. If you bought them frozen, throw them in the fridge overnight or just set them on the counter until they're room temp. It doesn't take too long—like 30 minutes or so. And have a damp kitchen towel handy so you can keep the wrappers moist while you're wrapping. If they dry out, they'll crack while you're rolling.

4 Set out a bowl of water next to the wrappers. You'll use this to seal the dumplings. I know some people who mix beaten egg or egg white with the water, but I like to keep it simple. And water works.

5 Finally, your filling. You'll want a bowl of it all mixed up and ready to go. Set this bowl after your wrappers and bowl of water and before your pan. It's easiest to work with cold filling, so if you can, make it ahead of time and refrigerate it until you're ready to start wrapping. Have a spoon, measuring tablespoon, butter knife, small offset spatula, or a pair of chopsticks ready for scooping the filling.

**1**

Take out five wrappers
and cover the rest
with a damp towel.

**2**

Lay out the five wrappers
like ducks in a row.

**3**

½"

Wet ½ inch (12 mm) of
the rim of each wrapper

**4**

FAT TEASPOON

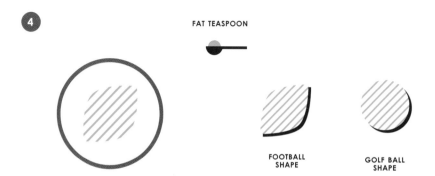

FOOTBALL
SHAPE

GOLF BALL
SHAPE

Scoop a fat teaspoon of
filling into the center of
each wrapper.

It's easier to fold the
wrapping around a football
shape than a golf ball shape.

**5**

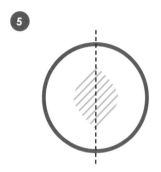

Fold at the dotted line
like a taco and pinch the
edges at the top center.

**6**

Choose your fold.

Good job!

# IT'S A WRAP

**1** Open the wrapper packet, take out five, and cover the rest with a damp towel.

**2** Lay out the wrappers like ducks in a row.

**3** Dip your finger in the water and wet ½ inch (12 mm) of the rim of each wrapper. You want it moister than a licked envelope, but not actually wet. The water will get the wrapper to stick to itself later, but too wet and it'll make the wrapper soggy and unfoldable.

**4** Scoop a fat teaspoon (basically a level tablespoon) of filling into the center of each wrapper. You can sorta eyeball it once you measure out one. The more filling you use, the harder it is to wrap, but the more satisfying the dumpling is. If you're new at this, start with a little less filling. I like to scoop the filling with a regular spoon and push it off so that it ends up in a tiny football shape. It's easier to fold the wrapping around this than a golf ball shape.

**5** Pick up one wrapper with the filling and cup it in your nondominant hand. With your dominant hand, fold the wrapper in half to enclose the filling and pinch the edges at the top center to seal. The edges should be lined up. If the water's dried up, dab it with a little more to moisten it enough to seal.

**6** Now, choose your fold! (See next page.)

# TYPES OF FOLDS

This is the fun part! However you fold them, the goal is to make sure your little dumplings are sealed tightly. You want that hermetic seal because it will allow the filling to cook inside the wrapper more effectively. Have fun and try all of the shapes!

HALF-MOON

Let's start with the simplest fold, which is best for boiling dumplings, when you don't need them to sit up in a pan.

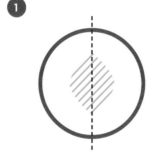

**1**

Fold at the dotted line.

**2**

Keep sealing the edges of the wrapper, moving out from the center, until they're sealed to the ends.

These look beautiful floating in soups.

**3**

Make sure the edges are really stuck together.

I love this
for Szechuan
Wontons
in Chili Oil
(page 38)!

TORTELLINI

The Italians got pasta
from the Chinese and now
I'm borrowing back their
stuffed-noodle fold.

HOT,
hot sauce
can cling
to the
folds.

**1**

Start with
the Half-Moon.

**2**

Dab a little water on the
two corners, then fold one
side toward the center

**3**

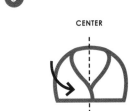

Fold the other side
to the center.

**4**

Press the ends together
to seal. The filled center
will plump up like a belly
with the edges framing it
like a bonnet.

**V-FOLD**

A step up from the Half-Moon, this technique gives you a dumpling that can sit flat in a pan.

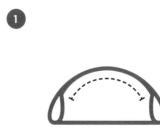

**1**

Keep sealing from the center out toward the ends until you have a ½-inch- (12-mm-) long opening at each end (each opening will be shaped like a teardrop).

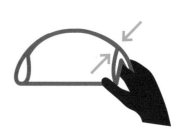

**2**

Take your index finger and push the rounded bottom of the teardrop up to meet the sealed pointed end and press to seal the end into a flat flap.

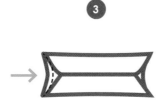

**3**

Do the same on the other side—the motion is sorta like dealing with the corners when wrapping a present.

---

**CRESCENT MOON**

This is the smiling version of the Half-Moon.

**1**

Start with the Half-Moon (you can also use the V-Fold).

**2**

Gently curve the dumpling into a crescent shape by pulling the ends toward each other.

The Curvy S is the slick, sleek sister of the Half-Moon.

**1** Start with the Half-Moon (you can also use the V-fold).

**2** Using your thumb and index finger on both sides, gently twist the dumpling's fin, the flat sealed rim, into an "S" shape.

---

BUDDHA'S BELLY

PLEAT

**1** Pinch the top center closed. With your left thumb and index finger holding the center together, use your right thumb and index finger to bring the front half of the wrapper facing you in toward the center.

**2** This will create a pleat that lines up with the folded part of the wrapper with the top edge.

**3** Repeat on the other side, then pinch the edges to seal and close the ends with a V-Fold.

**4** You can pleat all the way down to the edges, too!

# FRY, FRY AGAIN

Perfectly fried dumplings are a beautiful thing!

Pan-fried dumplings are the best. There are so many awesome textures: The top fins have a great chewy bite with their doubled-up skin and the bottoms get super-crisp and browned. My technique combines steaming and frying using a single pan. So easy, right? (But if you're a steamed or boiled dumpling lover, I've got those techniques coming right up.)

**1** First, get the right pan. Choose a nonstick skillet with a lid that you can pick up easily with one hand because you're gonna need to flip it later. So well-seasoned cast-iron is great if you're jacked.

**2** Coat the bottom of the pan with oil. I like using canola oil or another neutral oil. For a 12-inch (30.5-cm) pan, that's about 2 tablespoons. The oil will pool in a nonstick pan, but will spread out later.

**3** Start arranging the dumplings belly-to-belly in supertight concentric circles in a rosette shape. You should have one outer ring, one inner ring, and a few in the middle.

**4** Add 3 tablespoons water to the pan, set over medium heat, and cover. By starting with a cold pan, you're not under any pressure to arrange those dumplings quickly. And you don't have to deal with the whole cold-water/hot-oil scary splatter.

**5** Just let them cook now, rotating the pan every once in a while if you know your stove's heat is uneven. Because there's hot oil and water mixed in there, you want to keep the lid on tight to avoid getting burned. Don't be scared of the popping you hear. That sound means the bottoms are getting nice and fried while the fillings and tops steam.

**6** What you're waiting for is the water to evaporate. When it does, the sound under the lid will change from bubbly pops to a pretty serious steady crackle. Lift the lid away from your face and peek to see if the pan's dry. If it is, take off the lid. If not, cover it again. This step takes about 7 minutes with fresh dumplings and about 10 minutes with frozen ones. If you're worried about whether they're cooked through, you can use a meat thermometer to take the temp of one (the USDA says 165°F/75°C is what you need for meat) or poke one open from the top and peek inside. Try not to cut it all the way and let the juices spill out, though.

**7** After you've uncovered the dumplings, turn off the stove. Jerk the pan a little to give it a good shake and see if the dumplings are stuck or if they slide a little. If they seem stuck, shake the pan a little more to unstick them or slide a spatula under them to separate them from the pan.

> You'll know they're done when the feet are *crispy* and *dark* with *sizzly crackles* at the "heels." The fin will be *al dente* and the belly *soft* and *translucent*.

**8** Center a heatproof plate that's bigger than the pan over the pan. Put on oven mitts to protect your hands. Holding the pan and the plate tightly, flip them both together. Do it fast! Lift off the pan and voilà! There are your gorgeous dumplings. It's a beautiful dumpling tarte tatin!

**9** Right when the dumplings are done, they'll be really stuck together. I'm totally fine with that and think it's fun to pry them apart. If you let them sit for 5 minutes or so though, they pull apart much more easily. And, at that point, the fillings aren't burn-your-mouth hot. If you've gotta do a lot of batches to serve them all at the same time, tent the plate loosely with foil and place in a 200°F (90°C) oven. I prefer to invite everyone into the kitchen and let 'em eat while I keep frying.

### STEAMING OR BOILING DUMPLINGS

If you want to steam your dumplings, just stick them in a single layer in a covered steamer basket over simmering water. They'll take about 8 minutes to cook through if they're fresh and 10 if they're frozen. If you want to boil them, pop them into simmering water and adjust the heat to maintain a steady simmer. Fresh ones will be ready in 6 minutes and frozen ones in 8 minutes.

# FIXING FAILS

Once you get the hang of making dumplings, you'll think, "Whoa! How have I never tried this before? It's so easy!" Before you get to that point though, you may encounter a few road bumps. Here's how I fix common fails:

**FAIL: CRACKED WRAPPERS**

**FIX:** Dump 'em! You want to keep the wrappers under a damp paper towel or kitchen towel while you're working because they can dry out easily. If they're dry or cracked, they can't return to soft and supple. Not even with Chapstick. You gotta just throw them out; even good ol' water won't make them pliable and moist again.

**FAIL: FILLING IS TOO WET**

**FIX:** Easiest thing to do is drain off the excess liquid. If it's still too wet, add a little cornstarch to soak up the liquid and turn it into yummy juices once the dumplings are cooked.

**FAIL: RIPPED WRAPPER**

**FIX:** Toss it! The last thing you want is a hole in your wrapper. You can't patch it up the way you do pie dough. But save the filling. I hate wasting food, so I scrape the filling out of the failed wrapper back into the filling bowl for my next attempt.

## FAIL: FILLING SPILLING OUT

**FIX:** If your filling is spilling out of your wrapped dumpling, you have overfilled. Just get rid of some filling and stick the remaining filling back in with your finger and seal it tight.

## FAIL: DUMPLINGS STUCK TO EACH OTHER

**FIX:** Wait it out. As the dumplings cool, they'll naturally separate from each other. If they stay glued to each other, your best bet is to shovel them all into your piehole.

## FAIL: DUMPLINGS STUCK TO THE PAN

**FIX:** First, use a nonstick pan. Seriously. That will solve all your problems. Next, don't hassle them while they cook. If they're still stuck, let them cool down a little first, then run a thin offset silicone or fish spatula between the edges of the dumpling and the pan. Wiggle it in there gently so you don't rip the dumplings, and keep easing it in to pry the dumplings off.

## FAIL: UNEVEN BROWNING WHILE FRYING

**FIX:** Just keep rotating the pan to get the bottom to brown evenly. If the bottoms are darkening too much before the filling and wrapper fins are cooked through, turn the heat down.

# CHAPTER 1

# DUMPLINGS

# CLASSIC PORK & CHINESE CHIVE DUMPLINGS

MAKES ABOUT 45 DUMPLINGS

These are my favorite, favorite dumplings. Out of all the dumplings in this book, these are the ones I could eat every day. I'm around dumplings all the time and I honestly never get sick of any of them, but these are the savory classics I go to when I'm hungry. Nibble on that!

1½ pounds (680 g) Napa cabbage, cored and very finely chopped

¼ cup (30 g) finely chopped onion

3½ teaspoons kosher salt

1 pound (455 g) fatty (80/20) ground pork

¼ cup (25 g) finely chopped scallions

¼ cup (12 g) chopped garlic chives

1 large egg, beaten

1 tablespoon cornstarch

1 tablespoon plus 1 teaspoon soy sauce

1½ teaspoons minced garlic

1 teaspoon minced peeled fresh ginger

1 teaspoon sesame oil

¾ teaspoon freshly ground black pepper

1 (1-pound/455-g) package round dumpling wrappers

Soy-Vinegar Dip (page 102)

1  In a fine-mesh colander, mix the cabbage, onion, and 2½ teaspoons salt. Let stand while you get everything else ready, at least 10 minutes. Grab handfuls of the stuff and squeeze as hard as you can to get rid of all the liquid.

2  Transfer the dried cabbage-onion mix to a large bowl and add the pork, scallions, chives, egg, cornstarch, soy sauce, garlic, ginger, sesame oil, pepper, and remaining 1 teaspoon salt. Use your hands to get everything evenly distributed and well-mixed. It's best to use your hands because you can get everything incorporated into the meat without making the pieces of meat too small.

3  If you have time, cover and refrigerate the filling until nice and cold, up to 2 days. The filling will be easier to spoon into your wrappers when it's chilled.

4  When you're ready to cook, follow the wrapping and frying instructions on pages 22 to 31. Serve the dumplings with the Soy-Vinegar Dip.

A NOTE ON CHOPPING: One of the first things my mom taught me was how to chop everything the right size for a stir-fry. That way, everything cooks evenly. Harder veggies should be chopped smaller and tender ones bigger. The same is true of dumpling fillings. You want all the veggies to cook to the right degree of doneness in the same amount of time. So, mince your ginger and garlic, but give your onion a fine chop and get your cabbage to a very fine chop in between.

# MOM'S CILANTRO & PORK DUMPLINGS

MAKES ABOUT 45 DUMPLINGS

Cilantro is really divisive. If you're one of those people who taste soap or dirt or something else gross when you have cilantro, skip this one. If you're like my mom, a die-hard cilantro lover, read on. My mom puts whole bunches of the herb in, stems and all. The leaves are tasty, but the stems hold the strong herbaceous flavor. Just be sure to chop 'em up finely so they don't poke through the wrappers.

1 pound (455 g) Napa cabbage, cored and very finely chopped

2¼ teaspoons kosher salt

1 pound (455 g) fatty (80/20) ground pork

1 bunch cilantro, finely chopped

¼ cup (25 g) chopped scallions

2 tablespoons minced peeled fresh ginger

2 tablespoons soy sauce

1 tablespoon minced garlic

1 tablespoon sesame oil

½ teaspoon cornstarch

¼ teaspoon freshly ground black pepper

1 (1-pound/455-g) package round dumpling wrappers

Soy-Vinegar Dip (page 102)

1 In a fine-mesh colander, mix the cabbage and 2 teaspoons salt . Let stand while you get every-thing else ready, at least 10 minutes. Grab hand-fuls of the cabbage and squeeze as hard as you can to get rid of all the liquid.

2 Transfer the dried cabbage to a large bowl and add the pork, cilantro, scallions, ginger, soy sauce, garlic, sesame oil, cornstarch, pepper, and remaining ¼ teaspoon salt. Use your hands to work all the ingredients together until well-mixed. It's best to use your hands because you can get everything incorporated into the meat without making the pieces of meat too small.

3 If you have time, cover and refrigerate the filling until nice and cold, up to 2 days. The filling will be easier to spoon into your wrappers when it's chilled.

4 When you're ready to cook, follow the wrapping and frying instructions on pages 22 to 31. Serve the dumplings with the Soy-Vinegar Dip.

In Mandarin, *cilantro* is *xiang tsai*, which means "aromatic vegetable." Spot-on translation, right?

# SZECHUAN WONTONS IN CHILI OIL

MAKES ABOUT 45 DUMPLINGS

These slippery little suckers are lip smacking! This is one of those dishes that you crave from Szechuan restaurants, and now you can make it at home. Wear a bib or take your shirt off for these. I can never manage to keep the garlicky and numbingly spicy sauce from dripping onto my clothes while I'm shoveling these into my mouth.

**FOR THE CHUNKY CHILI OIL:**
1 tablespoon Szechuan pepper-corns, toasted
1 teaspoon fennel seeds, toasted
¾ cup (180 ml) peanut oil
¼ cup (60 ml) coconut oil
¼ cup (10 g) finely chopped dried Chinese red chiles

2 garlic cloves, peeled and smashed
Kosher salt

**FOR THE DUMPLINGS:**
1 pound (455 g) fatty (80/20) ground pork
1 large egg, beaten
1 tablespoon Shaoxing wine

1 teaspoon sesame oil
½ teaspoon kosher salt
¼ teaspoon grated fresh ginger
¼ cup (60 ml) Chicken Consommé (page 51) or canned lower-sodium chicken broth
1 (1-pound/455-g) package round dumpling wrappers

1   **Make the chunky chili oil:** Coarsely grind the peppercorns and fennel seeds using a mortar and pestle or spice grinder. Heat the peanut and coconut oils in a small saucepan over medium heat until hot but not smoking. Add the chiles, garlic, and peppercorn mixture. As soon as the chiles turn a darker shade of red, remove the pan from the heat. Let the oil cool completely, then season with salt to taste. The oil can be refrig-erated in an airtight container for up to 2 weeks. Bring to room temperature before using.

2   **Make the dumplings:** In a large bowl, combine the pork, egg, wine, sesame oil, salt, and ginger. Use your hands to work all the ingredients together until well-mixed. It's best to use your hands be-cause you can get everything incorporated into the meat without making the pieces of meat too small. Add the consommé and fold it in with your hands until just incorporated.

3   If you have time, cover and refrigerate the filling until nice and cold, up to 2 days. The filling will be easier to spoon into your wrappers when it's chilled.

4   When you're ready to cook, follow the wrapping instructions on pages 22 to 29, using the tortellini fold. Boil the dumplings in salted water until the skins wrinkle and the filling cooks through, about 6 minutes. Drain and immediately transfer to a large bowl and add the chili oil. Gently toss until the dumplings are well-coated. Divide among serving dishes and pour the chili oil from the bowl on top.

If you're serving these to guests with different levels of heat tolerance, pass the chili oil at the table instead. That way, everyone can get the dose they want.

The chili oil is also amazing on top of noodles, eggs, or anything else that you want to kick up a notch. Just be ready to sweat!

# PORK & CRAB DUMPLINGS

MAKES ABOUT 45 DUMPLINGS

Crab's one of those awesome ingredients that tastes really light and rich at the same time. That's doubly true when it's used in this filling. The meat—and you've gotta splurge on the good stuff here—breaks up the denser pork for a supple, loose filling. And that silky, crabby texture tastes super rich, even though it's low in fat. It's the best of both worlds here.

1 pound (455 g) fatty (80/20) ground pork

1 pound (455 g) backfin crab meat, picked through for cartilage

1 large egg white

2 tablespoons snipped chives

1 teaspoon minced peeled fresh ginger

¼ teaspoon kosher salt

¼ teaspoon freshly ground black pepper

1 (1-pound/455-g) package round dumpling wrappers

Vinegar-Ginger Dip (page 102)

1   In a large bowl, combine the pork, crab, egg white, chives, ginger, salt, and pepper. Use your hands to work all the ingredients together until well-mixed. It's best to use your hands because you can get everything incorporated into the meat without making the pieces of meat too small.

2   If you have time, cover and refrigerate the filling until nice and cold, up to 2 days. The filling will be easier to spoon into your wrappers when it's chilled.

3   When you're ready to cook, follow the wrapping and frying instructions on pages 22 to 31. Serve the dumplings with the Vinegar-Ginger Dip.

Did you know a Japanese Spider Crab can span up to 12 feet (3.6 m) claw to claw? That's a lot of pork & crab dumplings!

DON'T BE CRABBY!

# PORK & SHRIMP DUMPLINGS

MAKES ABOUT 45 DUMPLINGS

You know a Chinese joint is classy when they have fat pieces of shrimp in their dumplings. And I'm all class. My take on this dumpling is so luxurious: Shrimp is finely chopped in the filling, then a fat nub goes on top right before wrapping. The orangey-pink chunks create hilly humps under the dumpling skin and give you something to chew on in each bite.

24 extra-large (26/30-count) shrimp, shelled and deveined
12 ounces (340 g) fatty (80/20) ground pork
2 teaspoons minced shallot

2 teaspoons soy sauce
2 teaspoons rice wine
1 teaspoon minced peeled fresh ginger
¼ teaspoon kosher salt

½ teaspoon freshly ground black pepper
1 (1-pound/455-g) package round dumpling wrappers
Toasted Sesame—Soy Dip (page 103)

If you can find "never frozen" shrimp (usually from a Gulf coast catch) at a reliable fish counter, go for it! Otherwise, buy frozen. Shrimp usually arrives at the market frozen and is thawed there. Might as well defrost it yourself at home!

Shrimp is sold by count per pound. Rather than look for the "extra-large" label, be sure to get 26/30-count, which means there are that many in a pound. The smaller the shrimp, the higher the count per pound.

1 Cut 15 shrimp into thirds crosswise; cover and refrigerate. Finely chop the remaining 9 shrimp and transfer to a large bowl along with the pork, shallot, soy sauce, wine, ginger, salt, and pepper. Use your hands to work all the ingredients together until well-mixed. It's best to use your hands because you can get everything incorporated into the meat without making the pieces of meat too small.

2 If you have time, cover and refrigerate the filling until nice and cold, up to 2 days. The filling will be easier to spoon into your wrappers when it's chilled.

3 When you're ready to cook, follow the wrapping instructions on pages 22 to 29, filling each wrapper with ½ tablespoon of the dumpling filling and pressing 1 piece shrimp on top before enclosing. Steam or fry them according to the instructions on page 30. Serve the dumplings with the Toasted Sesame—Soy Dip.

# THAI GREEN CURRY DUMPLINGS

MAKES ABOUT 45 DUMPLINGS

One of my favorite cookbooks of all time is *Hot Sour Salty Sweet* by Jeffrey Alford and Naomi Duguid, and one of my favorite recipes in there is their green curry paste. I've adapted their formula to work in a dumpling filling that's flavorful enough to stand on its own. If you're a total chile head, you can add even more of the green chiles or dip it in chile sauce.

1 pound (455 g) Napa cabbage, cored and finely chopped

2¼ teaspoons kosher salt

1 pound (455 g) fatty (80/20) ground pork

1 tablespoon minced fresh lemongrass

1 tablespoon minced peeled fresh galangal or ginger

1 tablespoon minced shallot

1½ teaspoons coriander seeds, toasted and ground

1 teaspoon freshly grated lime zest

1 teaspoon minced fresh green Thai chile

½ teaspoon freshly ground black pepper

1 (1-pound/455-g) package round dumpling wrappers

Dr. Tan's Chile Dip (page 104; optional)

1   In a fine-mesh colander, mix the cabbage and 2 teaspoons salt. Let stand while you get every-thing else ready, at least 10 minutes. Grab hand-fuls of the cabbage and squeeze as hard as you can to get rid of all the liquid.

2   Transfer the dried cabbage to a large bowl and add the pork, lemongrass, galangal or ginger, shallot, coriander, lime zest, chile, pepper, and remaining ¼ teaspoon salt. Use your hands to work all the ingredients together until well-mixed. It's best to use your hands because you can get everything incorporated into the meat without making the pieces of meat too small.

3   If you have time, cover and refrigerate the filling until nice and cold, up to 2 days. The filling will be easier to spoon into your wrappers when it's chilled.

4   When you're ready to cook, follow the wrapping and frying instructions on pages 22 to 31. Serve the dumplings with Dr. Tan's Chile Dip, if desired.

Curry—basically cooking ingredients in a mix of strong spices—started out as a way to preserve food and make less-than-fresh ingredients taste great.

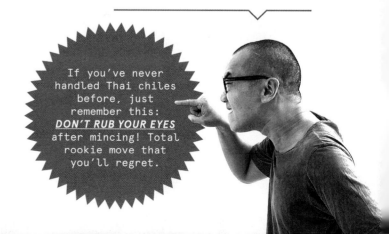

If you've never handled Thai chiles before, just remember this: *DON'T RUB YOUR EYES* after mincing! Total rookie move that you'll regret.

# THE
# SECRET
## TO
# 10-MINUTE
# DINNERS

Yeah, dumplings take time to wrap and fold. That's why I'm all about making way more than I'm gonna eat in a sitting. They taste great when you cook them straight from the freezer and only need a few more minutes in the pan or steamer. On those nights when you don't feel like cooking, going to a restaurant, or ordering take-out, you can throw some frozen dumplings on the stove and be ready to eat a full meal in less than 10 minutes.

1. Start by putting completed dumplings on a parchment paper–lined pan that will fit in your freezer. Space them 1 to 2 inches (2.5 to 5 cm) apart so they don't stick to each other.

2. Freeze them until they're hard as rocks.

3. Label plastic freezer bags with the name of the dumpling and the date they were made, then pop in the frozen dumplings. Be sure to squeeze all the air out of the bag before sealing! No one likes freezer burn. They will keep for up to 6 months.

4. Frozen dumplings make the best gift for friends and family who need a stash of ready-to-cook food—new mommas and papas, bachelor buddies, grandparents and great-grands. Just wrap up the plastic bags and deliver!

USE A
TOWEL
TO HOLD
THE PAN

LOOK
AT THAT
GLAZE!

# GLAZED BARBECUED PORK DUMPLINGS

MAKES ABOUT 45 DUMPLINGS

All the fruity sugars of my barbecue sauce turn into this sticky finger-lickin' glaze when cooked onto barbecued ribs. It made me wonder: Why couldn't I get the same effect with dumplings? Guess what? I can. And did. I stuffed my fave barbecue plate combo—pork and slaw—into the dumplings, then threw some sauce in the pan while they fried. The sauce does double duty here, seasoning the meat filling and caramelizing into an amazing crust. Use extra sauce as a dip and it goes triple duty!

8 ounces (225 g) red cabbage, very finely chopped
2¼ teaspoons kosher salt
1 pound (455 g) fatty (80/20) ground pork

2 tablespoons rendered bacon fat
½ teaspoon freshly ground black pepper

Asian Barbecue Sauce (page 109)
1 (1-pound/455-g) package round dumpling wrappers

1   In a fine-mesh colander, mix the cabbage and 2 teaspoons salt. Let stand while you get everything else ready, at least 10 minutes. Grab handfuls of the cabbage and squeeze as hard as you can to get rid of all the liquid.

2   Transfer the dried cabbage to a large bowl and add the pork, bacon fat, pepper, ½ cup (120 ml) barbecue sauce, and remaining ¼ teaspoon salt. Use your hands to work all the ingredients together until well-mixed. It's best to use your hands because you can get everything incorporated into the meat without making the pieces of meat too small. Stir ¼ cup (60 ml) water into the remaining sauce.

3   If you have time, cover and refrigerate the filling until nice and cold, up to 2 days. The filling will be easier to spoon into your wrappers when it's chilled.

4   When you're ready to cook, follow the wrapping and frying instructions on pages 22 to 31. For each batch you fry, drizzle in enough of the remaining sauce to coat the bottom of the pan during the last 2 minutes of cooking. The sauce will caramelize onto the dumplings. Wash and dry the pan between batches. Flip the dumplings out of the pan and serve them right away for the crispest glazed crust.

Having trouble imagining barbecue sauce caramelized onto dumplings? Think savory, meaty tarte tatin. Now, stop drooling all over this page.

# MA PO TOFU DUMPLINGS

MAKES ABOUT 45 DUMPLINGS

During my college semester studying abroad in China, I ate everywhere with Bridget, my best friend and fellow food lover. When she first arrived in China, she was a vegetarian. Oh, how things quickly changed. Before she switched to being an omnivore, she would ask whether there was meat in the ma po tofu whenever we found it on a menu. And the waiters always replied, "There's just a little bit of pork." Bridget convinced herself—even tried to convince *me*—that the tiny crumbles in the dish were actually broken up tofu and not pork. I knew the truth and I still know it now. It's the ratio of pork to tofu that makes ma po tofu so great. This is one of those vegetarian-carnivore crossover dishes that make meat-lovers heart tofu and vegetarians turn a blind eye.

4 ounces (115 g) fatty (80/20) ground pork
¼ teaspoon kosher salt
1 teaspoon minced garlic
1 pound (455 g) soft tofu, patted dry and finely diced

½ cup (50 g) thinly sliced scallions
3 tablespoons chili oil
2 teaspoons *dobujang* (fermented soy bean paste)
1 teaspoon Szechuan peppercorns, toasted and crushed

½ teaspoon sugar
¼ teaspoon crushed red chile flakes
1 (1-pound/455-g) package round dumpling wrappers
Vinegar-Ginger Dip (page 102; optional)

1   Heat a medium skillet over medium-high heat. Add the pork and season with the salt. Cook, stirring and breaking the meat into tiny bits, until browned, about 5 minutes. Add the garlic and cook, stirring and scraping the pan, for 1 minute. Transfer the mixture to a large bowl.

2   Add the tofu, scallions, chili oil, *dobujang*, peppercorns, sugar, and chile flakes. With a silicone spatula, gently fold all the ingredients together until evenly mixed.

3   If you have time, cover and refrigerate the filling until nice and cold, up to 2 days. The filling will be easier to spoon into your wrappers when it's chilled.

4   When you're ready to cook, follow the wrapping and frying instructions on pages 22 to 31. Serve the dumplings with the Vinegar-Ginger Dip, if desired.

You like ma po tofu for take-out? This is the best way to get it to go!

# WHEAT FLOUR WRAPPERS

MAKES 20 WRAPPERS

It's no secret that I use store-bought wrappers. They work well, create a consistent product, and taste great. The one thing they can't do is encase soup dumplings. For the tidal wave of soup that's stuffed into the Shanghainese specialty, the wrapper has to come up around the sides of the filling and be pinched shut in a top knot so that the sides are seamless. For that to happen, the wrapper must be fresh and supple enough to stretch and stick to itself. If you're into kneading and rolling dough, you should definitely tackle this project. Even if you don't want to go all the way and do soup dumplings, you can use these wrappers for any of the fillings in this chapter. The only difference is that you won't need to pleat the soft dough; you can just pinch the edges together.

2½ cups (363 grams) all-purpose flour, plus more for rolling

¾ cup (180 ml) hot (but not boiling) water

1 tablespoon vegetable oil
¼ cup (60 ml) cold water

1  Place the flour in a large bowl. Start stirring with chopsticks and continue stirring while you add the hot water in a steady stream. Keep stirring while adding the oil and the cold water in a steady stream. Knead the dough in the bowl until all the bits of flour stick to the dough mass.

2  Transfer the dough to a lightly floured surface and knead, adding flour if the dough gets too sticky, until smooth and elastic, about 8 minutes. When you poke the dough, it should bounce back. Wrap in plastic wrap and let rest at room temperature for 30 minutes.

# HOW TO MAKE
## SOUP DUMPLINGS

**1**

Have the Wheat Flour Wrappers dough (page 47) and one of the soup dumpling fillings (pages 52 to 54) ready to go.

**2**

Cut the dough in half and keep half covered. Roll the uncovered half into a log and cut into ten equal pieces.

**6**

Place 1 tablespoon filling in the center of the wrapper.

**7**

Dab a little water around the edges.

**8**

Pick up four "corners" of the wrapper and pull them in toward the center so the filling can settle into the base.

DON'T GET MAD, GET STEAMED!

**12**

Fill a wok with water to a depth of 3 inches (7.5 cm) or so. You basically want as much water as you can get in there without it touching the bottom of the steamer, so pop the steamer on the wok and add or remove water as needed. Bring the water to a boil.

**13**

Meanwhile, line two bamboo steamers with Napa cabbage leaves or strips of parchment paper. Place the dumplings on top, spacing 2 inches (5 cm) apart. Steam until the wrappers and fillings are cooked through, 6 to 7 minutes. If your wrappers are thin enough, you should see the soup bubbling inside. Serve in the steamer, instructing guests to very carefully pick up the dumplings with chopsticks.

**3**

Working with one piece of dough at a time and keeping the others covered with plastic wrap, roll the dough into a very thin 5-inch (12-cm) round on a lightly floured surface. A small dowel works best for this.

**4**

You want to roll from the center out, keeping a quarter-sized pad of thicker dough in the middle, and turning the dough with each roll to get an even circle.

**5**

With your left hand, rotate the skin as you roll it out with your right hand. The edges should end up really thin so that they don't get clumpy when you pleat them at the top of the dumpling.

**9**

Pleat the wrapper between the corners to enclose the filling, then pinch the dough together right above the filling, where all the pleats meet.

**10**

This is the hard part so concentrate now! Press the dough above the pinched center to flatten the edges to resemble a tiny flower.

**11**

Place on a parchment-lined half-sheet pan. Repeat with the remaining dough and filling.

---

### PRO TIPS 👆

- Any flat-bottomed steamer works, but bamboo is the best. It not only holds heat really well, but it also imparts a nice woodsy aroma to the food. And it makes you look like an authentic pro.

- Before wrapping, keep the filling chilled so it stays thick, which makes it easier to scoop.

- Napa cabbage leaves are the best nonstick liner for soup dumplings. You want to use the top frilly parts, which have a webbiness ideal for letting through steam. The leaves allow you to gently pick the dumplings out of the steamer without ripping the skins. Bonus: The leaves soak up all the dumpling juices. Be sure to eat them as a tasty side dish.

# THE
# ART
## OF
# EATING
# SOUP
# DUMPLINGS

At a young age, I was told that it's bad luck to let any precious soup drip out of the dumpling. The way you eat soup dumplings is as important as the way you prepare them. Follow these three steps to soup dumpling nirvana:

**1** Gently pick up a dumpling with the sides of chopsticks (the tips could poke a hole!) and sit it in a Chinese soupspoon. Take a small nibble from the skin to make a hole. Careful! The steam shooting out will be hot!

**2** Slowly sip some of the soup out of the hole you've just made. Blow first if it's way too hot. You don't want to burn your tongue.

**3** I like to use a narrow spoon to put a bit of the vinegar sauce into the hole to mingle with the soup inside. Now go for it!

# CHICKEN CONSOMMÉ

The secret to soup dumplings is this jellied chicken stock. Chicken wings naturally make stock gelatinous, but powdered gelatin helps it set even further. The solid stock gets folded into the fillings, then becomes that signature burst of soup inside the wrappers when the dumplings are steamed.

3 pounds (1.4 kg) chicken wings

4 ounces (115 g) Smithfield ham

1 cup (100 g) sliced scallions, white parts only

2 ounces (55 g) sliced peeled fresh ginger

3 dried shiitake mushrooms

1 large garlic clove, peeled

1 tablespoon mushroom soy sauce

2 teaspoons Shaoxing wine

2 (¼-ounce/10-g) packets powdered unflavored gelatin

¼ cup (60 ml) cold water

Mix any leftover consommé with ground meat for the juiciest meatballs or burgers you've ever had!

1   In a large stockpot, combine the chicken wings, ham, scallions, ginger, mushrooms, garlic, soy sauce, wine, and 10 cups (2.5 L) water. Bring to a boil over high heat, skimming off any foam that rises to the surface, then reduce the heat to maintain a steady simmer. Simmer for 2 hours, replenishing the water if it falls below the line of the solids in the pot.

2   In a small bowl, sprinkle the gelatin over the cold water. Remove the stock from the heat and stir in the gelatin mixture until it dissolves. Strain the stock through a sieve, pressing on the solids to extract as much liquid as possible. Discard the solids.

3   Refrigerate the stock in airtight containers until cold and set, at least 4 hours and up to 5 days.

# PORK SHANGHAI SOUP DUMPLINGS

―――――――――――――――――――――

MAKES ABOUT 20 DUMPLINGS

Pure and simple—that's how I like my soup dumpling fillings. This classic pork mix reminds me of all the soup dumpling shops I've hit over my lifetime, from California to Asia to New York. Some cooks keep the consommé separate from the filling, placing cubes of it on top of the meat. I like folding the consommé into the filling because it loosens up the meat and permeates it with its yumminess and still gives you a rich broth inside the wrapper.

8 ounces (225 g) fatty (80/20) ground pork
2 tablespoons minced scallions
1 tablespoon soy sauce
2 teaspoons Shaoxing wine

1 teaspoon sugar
1 teaspoon minced peeled fresh ginger
½ teaspoon minced garlic
½ teaspoon sesame oil
¼ teaspoon kosher salt

¾ cup (180 ml) Chicken Consommé (page 51)
Napa cabbage leaves, for steaming
Wheat Flour Wrappers (page 47)
Vinegar-Ginger Dip (page 102)

1  In a large bowl, combine the pork, scallions, soy sauce, wine, sugar, ginger, garlic, sesame oil, and salt. Use your hands to work all the ingredients together until well-mixed. It's best to use your hands because you can get everything incorporated into the meat without making the pieces of meat too small. Add the consommé and fold it in with your hands just until evenly distributed.

2  Cover and refrigerate the filling until cold and firm, at least 5 minutes and up to 2 days. The filling will be easier to spoon into your wrappers when it's chilled.

3  When you're ready to cook, follow the instructions on pages 48 to 49.

4  Serve the dumplings immediately with the Vinegar-Ginger Dip.

# SHRIMP SOUP DUMPLINGS

MAKES ABOUT 20 DUMPLINGS

I love the brashness of Asian cuisine. Mixing precious shrimp with flavor-forward pork is such a splurge, but so called for in this soup dumpling. This seafood-meets-meat filling is super luxurious. The taste of the shrimp when it mixes with the broth is the ultimate!

2½ ounces (70 g) peeled and deveined shrimp
8 ounces (225 g) fatty (80/20) ground pork
3 tablespoons minced scallions
2 tablespoons minced onion

1 tablespoon sugar
1 tablespoon soy sauce
1½ teaspoons minced garlic
1½ teaspoons rice wine vinegar
¼ teaspoon sesame oil
¼ teaspoon kosher salt

1¼ cups (300 ml) Chicken Consommé (page 51)
Napa cabbage leaves, for steaming
Wheat Flour Wrappers (page 47)
Soy-Vinegar Dip (page 102)

1 Pulse the shrimp in a food processor until finely ground. Transfer to a large bowl and add the pork, scallions, onion, sugar, soy sauce, garlic, vinegar, sesame oil, and salt. Use your hands to work all the ingredients together until well-mixed. It's best to use your hands because you can get everything incorporated into the meat without making the pieces of meat too small. Add the consommé and gently fold in with your hands just until evenly distributed.

2 Cover and refrigerate the filling until cold and firm, at least 5 minutes and up to 2 days. The filling will be easier to spoon into your wrappers when it's chilled.

3 When you're ready to cook, follow the instructions on pages 48 to 49.

4 Serve the dumplings immediately with the Soy-Vinegar Dip.

# HOT & SOUR SOUP DUMPLINGS

MAKES ABOUT 20 DUMPLINGS

When I crave a little more kick to the soup gushing out of my dumplings, I turn to this recipe. The spices and seasonings in the filling infuse the soup with flavor while the dumplings steam.

8 ounces (225 g) fatty (80/20) ground pork
2 tablespoons minced scallions
1 tablespoon Shaoxing wine
1 tablespoon soy sauce
2 teaspoons Chinese black vinegar

1 teaspoon sugar
1 teaspoon minced peeled fresh ginger
½ teaspoon minced garlic
½ teaspoon chili oil
¼ teaspoon kosher salt
⅛ teaspoon cayenne pepper

1 cup (240 ml) Chicken Consommé (page 51)
Napa cabbage leaves, for steaming
Wheat Flour Wrappers (page 47)
Vinegar-Ginger Dip (page 102)

1   In a large bowl, combine the pork, scallions, wine, soy sauce, vinegar, sugar, ginger, garlic, chili oil, salt, and cayenne. Use your hands to work all the ingredients together until well-mixed. It's best to use your hands because you can get everything incorporated into the meat without making the pieces of meat too small. Add the consommé and gently fold it in with your hands just until evenly distributed.

2   Cover and refrigerate the filling until cold and firm, at least 5 minutes and up to 2 days. The filling will be easier to spoon into your wrappers when it's chilled.

3   When you're ready to cook, follow the instructions on pages 48 to 49.

4   Serve the dumplings immediately with the Vinegar-Ginger Dip.

"Spicy soup dumplings make me want to give myself a high five."

# WATERCRESS BEEF DUMPLINGS

MAKES ABOUT 45 DUMPLINGS

Watercress packs a bright, sharp bite that balances the beefiness of this filling. I love this combo of fresh green veg and meaty meat. To keep the texture of the filling light, I mix in slippery, soft mung bean noodles.

1 bundle (50 g) vermicelli mung bean noodles
1 pound (455 g) ground beef chuck
2 cups (170 g) finely chopped fresh watercress, plus more for garnish
1 tablespoon finely chopped garlic
¼ cup (60 ml) oyster sauce
½ teaspoon kosher salt
1 (1-pound/455-g) package round dumpling wrappers
Hoisin Dip (page 108)

Mung bean noodles are sometimes labeled "threads." Just be sure to buy the skinny round sticks and not the fatter ribbons.

One of the most unusual farms I've been to is Sumida Farms in Honolulu. The farmers wore T-shirts that say "Eat More Watercress." I agree!

1 Fill a medium bowl with ice and water. Bring a small pot of water to a boil and drop the noodles in. Cook just until softened, about 3 minutes, then drain and transfer to the ice water. When cool, drain again, then finely chop the noodles. Transfer 1 cup (175 g) chopped noodles to a large bowl and add the beef, watercress, garlic, oyster sauce, and salt. Reserve any remaining noodles for another use. Use your hands to work all the ingredients together until well-mixed. It's best to use your hands because you can get everything incorporated into the meat without making the pieces of meat too small.

2 If you have time, cover and refrigerate the filling until nice and cold, up to 2 days. The filling will be easier to spoon into your wrappers when it's chilled.

3 When you're ready to cook, follow the wrapping and frying instructions on pages 22 to 31.

4 Serve the dumplings with the Hoisin Dip and garnish with additional watercress.

# DUMPLINGS ARE
# NOT JUST ASIAN,
## MY FRIEND

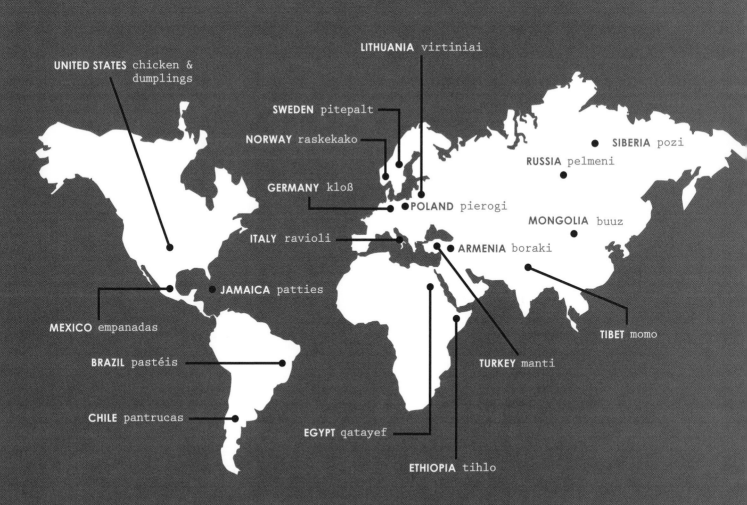

LITHUANIA virtiniai

UNITED STATES chicken & dumplings

SWEDEN pitepalt

NORWAY raskekako

GERMANY kloß

SIBERIA pozi

RUSSIA pelmeni

POLAND pierogi

MONGOLIA buuz

ITALY ravioli

ARMENIA boraki

JAMAICA patties

MEXICO empanadas

TIBET momo

BRAZIL pastéis

TURKEY manti

CHILE pantrucas

EGYPT qatayef

ETHIOPIA tihlo

# LEMONGRASS–LIME LEAF BEEF DUMPLINGS

MAKES ABOUT 45 DUMPLINGS

Even a few years ago, I had to hunt for kaffir lime leaves in specialty stores all over town. Now, they're available in many supermarkets! The glossy green leaves come in pairs and smell like a cross between citrus and eucalyptus. Lemongrass is another esoteric-to-everyday ingredient now. Its subtle lemony freshness adds a unique dimension to Southeast Asian cuisine. It lightens other flavors while asserting its own herbaceous fragrance. This pairing of lime leaves and lemongrass brings a fruity-grassy aroma to these easy dumplings.

1 pound (455 g) ground beef chuck
⅔ cup (17 g) fresh kaffir lime leaves, very thinly sliced
3 tablespoons minced fresh lemongrass

1 tablespoon plus 1 teaspoon finely chopped scallions
2 teaspoons minced garlic
2 teaspoons minced peeled fresh ginger
1 teaspoon fish sauce

½ teaspoon freshly grated lime zest
½ teaspoon kosher salt
1 (1-pound/455-g) package round dumpling wrappers
Dr. Tan's Chile Dip (page 104)

1  In a large bowl, combine the beef, lime leaves, lemongrass, scallions, garlic, ginger, fish sauce, lime zest, and salt. Use your hands to work all the ingredients together until well-mixed. It's best to use your hands because you can get everything incorporated into the meat without making the pieces of meat too small.

2  If you have time, cover and refrigerate the filling until nice and cold, up to 2 days. The filling will be easier to spoon into your wrappers when it's chilled.

3  When you're ready to cook, follow the wrapping and frying instructions on pages 22 to 31.

4  Serve the dumplings with Dr. Tan's Chile Dip.

Both lime leaves and lemongrass have stringy fibers. Be sure to finely cut them—the former into thin shreds, the latter into a mince—to get a hearty texture without a tough chewiness.

WHEN LIFE GIVES YOU LEMONGRASS, MAKE LEMONGRASS DUMPLINGS!

# SPICY BEEF & SHISO DUMPLINGS

You know those green leaves on sushi platters? The ones that look like maple leaves, but with saw-toothed edges and an almost fuzzy surface? They're totally edible. And really delicious. Shiso leaves taste like a cross between fennel and mint. I like them both cooked and fresh, so I mix them into the dumpling filling and use the whole leaves as tiny wraps for the dumplings.

1 pound (455 g) ground beef chuck
2 tablespoons minced garlic
3 tablespoons *gochujang* (Korean chile-bean paste)

16 fresh shiso leaves, finely chopped (4 teaspoons), plus 45 leaves for serving
1 tablespoon sesame oil
1 large egg, beaten

½ teaspoon kosher salt
1 (1-pound/455-g) package round dumpling wrappers

1   In a large bowl, combine the beef, garlic, *gochujang*, chopped shiso, sesame oil, egg, and salt. Use your hands to work all the ingredients together until well-mixed. It's best to use your hands because you can get everything incorporated into the meat without making the pieces of meat too small.

2   If you have time, cover and refrigerate the filling until nice and cold, up to 2 days. The filling will be easier to spoon into your wrappers when it's chilled.

3   When you're ready to cook, follow the wrapping and frying instructions on pages 22 to 31.

4   Separate the fried dumplings and wrap each in a shiso leaf to serve.

The shiso leaf
wrapper looks so
beautiful and makes
it easy for guests to
pick up dumplings
without getting
their fingers
dirty.

# KIMCHI BEEF DUMPLINGS

MAKES ABOUT 45 DUMPLINGS

*Mandoo!* I love that word! *Mandoo* is the Korean word for "dumpling." There are so many versions of Korean dumplings, but one of my favorites is filled with kimchi. The only problem is that store-bought kimchi varies so widely in quality and flavor. I decided to do my own fresh take on kimchi for these dumplings. I capture the garlicky heat of the classic, but forgo the fermented funk. Even without the pickled preserved edge, this filling's got big, big flavors.

1 pound (455 g) Napa cabbage,
  cored and finely chopped
2 teaspoons kosher salt
1 pound (455 g) ground beef
  chuck

1 cup (120 g) finely chopped
  onion
½ cup (120 ml) *gochujang*
  (Korean chile-bean paste)
2 tablespoons finely chopped
  garlic
1 tablespoon sugar

1 tablespoon sesame seeds
1 teaspoon soy sauce
⅛ teaspoon freshly ground
  black pepper
1 (1-pound/455-g) package
  round dumpling wrappers

1  In a fine-mesh colander, mix the cabbage and salt. Let stand while you get everything else ready, at least 10 minutes. Grab handfuls of the cabbage and squeeze as hard as you can to get rid of all the liquid.

2  Transfer the dried cabbage to a large bowl and add the beef, onion, *gochujang*, garlic, sugar, sesame seeds, soy sauce, and pepper. Use your hands to work all the ingredients together until well-mixed. It's best to use your hands because you can get everything incorporated into the meat without making the pieces of meat too small.

3  If you have time, cover and refrigerate the filling until nice and cold, up to 2 days. The filling will be easier to spoon into your wrappers when it's chilled.

4  When you're ready to cook, follow the wrapping and frying instructions on pages 22 to 31. Serve the dumplings hot.

Make more dumplings!

# CUMIN LAMB DUMPLINGS

MAKES ABOUT 45 DUMPLINGS

When I taste cumin and fennel, it takes me back to my days as a student in Beijing. Right behind our university was the Uighur neighborhood. Uighurs are Chinese nationals, but they come from the far west and are more closely associated with Mongolia. Among the Uighurs who moved to Beijing were the vendors who sold me lamb kebabs that were coated in smoky cumin and fennel. When I bit into a hot kebab, the seeds would pop in my mouth. I've stuffed those flavors into dumplings and lightened them up with peppers—both sweet and hot. A dunk in yogurt sauce adds another fresh note.

1 pound (455 g) ground lamb

¾ cup (113 g) finely diced red bell pepper

¼ cup (38 g) finely diced seeded jalapeño

1 tablespoon cumin seeds, toasted and coarsely ground (see Note)

2 teaspoons minced garlic

1½ teaspoons fennel seeds, toasted and coarsely ground (see Note)

1 teaspoon crushed red chile flakes

1 teaspoon kosher salt

1 (1-pound/455-g) package round dumpling wrappers

Lemon-Yogurt Dip (page 112)

Ground lamb shoulder tastes richer (yeah, I mean fattier) than ground leg of lamb, but both work here.

1 In a large bowl, combine the lamb, bell pepper, jalapeño, cumin seeds, garlic, fennel seeds, chile flakes, and salt. Use your hands to work all the ingredients together until well-mixed. It's best to use your hands because you can get everything incorporated into the meat without making the pieces of meat too small.

2 If you have time, cover and refrigerate the filling until nice and cold, up to 2 days. The filling will be easier to spoon into your wrappers when it's chilled.

3 When you're ready to cook, follow the wrapping and frying instructions on pages 22 to 31. Serve the dumplings with the Lemon-Yogurt Dip.

NOTE: To toast spices, heat them in a skillet over medium heat, tossing, until fragrant and just starting to pop out of the pan.

If you don't line your steamer with Napa cabbage, rub it with cooking oil to keep your lovely dumplings from sticking.

# CHICKEN & THAI BASIL DUMPLINGS

MAKES ABOUT 45 DUMPLINGS

You'll cross the road for this chicken. What's great about the combo is that it's all superauthentic Southeast Asian ingredients and flavors, but in a traditional Chinese dumpling shape. The depth of flavor from the lemongrass marinade in the chicken balances the bright top note of fresh basil. You're totally going to want to marry the Spicy Peanut Dip (page 106) that comes with it.

½ cup (100 g) sugar
¼ cup (60 ml) fish sauce
2 garlic cloves
1 lemongrass stalk, trimmed, smashed, and coarsely chopped
2 teaspoons freshly ground black pepper

1 bundle (50 g) vermicelli mung bean noodles
1 pound (455 g) ground chicken (see Note)
1 cup (130 g) very finely chopped carrots
¼ cup (6 g) thinly sliced Thai basil leaves
¼ cup (25 g) finely chopped scallions

1 tablespoon plus 2 teaspoons kosher salt
2¼ teaspoons sriracha
2¼ teaspoons fresh lime juice
1 tablespoon cornstarch
1 (1-pound/455-g) package round dumpling wrappers
Spicy Peanut Dip (page 106)

1 In a food processor, combine the sugar, fish sauce, garlic, lemongrass, and 1¼ teaspoons pepper. Pulse until the lemongrass is very finely chopped. Transfer the marinade to an airtight container and refrigerate at least overnight and up to 1 week.

2 When ready to cook, strain the marinade through a fine-mesh sieve, pressing on the solids to extract as much liquid as possible. You should have ½ cup (120 ml). (If you have extra, save it to use as a marinade for grilling chicken, pork, or beef.)

3 Fill a medium bowl with ice and water. Bring a small pot of water to a boil and drop the noodles in. Cook just until softened, about 3 minutes, then drain and transfer to the ice water. When cool, drain again, then chop the noodles.

4 In a large bowl, combine the chicken, carrots, basil, scallions, salt, sriracha, lime juice, corn-

starch, ½ cup (120 ml) marinade, noodles, and remaining ¾ teaspoon pepper. Use your hands to work all the ingredients together until well-mixed. It's best to use your hands because you can get everything incorporated into the meat without making the pieces of meat too small.

5 If you have time, cover and refrigerate the filling until nice and cold, up to 2 days. The filling will be easier to spoon into your wrappers when it's chilled.

6 When you're ready to cook, follow the wrapping and frying instructions on pages 22 to 31. Serve the dumplings with the Spicy Peanut Dip.

NOTE: For the chicken, I prefer a blend of 70 percent white meat and 30 percent dark meat. Your best bet is to ask a butcher to grind the meat for you. The prepacked stuff tends to be a little pasty.

# SZECHUAN CHICKEN DUMPLINGS

MAKES ABOUT 75 DUMPLINGS

We're talking hard-hitting flavors here. Szechuan food isn't just straight-up spicy, even though it's best known for the heat of its dishes. Its cuisine is also sour from pickles, savory and sweet from soy in all its forms, and fresh from aromatics like scallions, garlic, and ginger. And, of course, there's the signature tingle of Szechuan peppercorns. That numbing sensation makes it really addictive. Once you stock your pantry with the Szechuan seasonings and sauces for these dumplings, you can pretty much nail any other Szechuan dish you want to try.

¾ cup (150 g) dried white soybeans
Cold water, as needed
Kosher salt
½ cup (52 g) bean sprouts
4 ounces (115 g) extra-firm tofu, drained well
1 pound (455 g) ground dark-meat chicken

¾ cup (75 g) thinly sliced scallions
3 tablespoons Chinese bean sauce (see Note)
2 tablespoons Szechuan chili sauce (see Note)
1 tablespoon finely chopped Szechuan pickles (see Note)
1 large egg yolk
1 teaspoon minced garlic

1 teaspoon sesame oil
½ teaspoon minced peeled fresh ginger
½ teaspoon freshly ground black pepper
½ teaspoon cornstarch
1½ (1-pound/455-g) packages round dumpling wrappers

Szechuan Peppercorns were illegal in the United States from 1968 to 2005 because of a fear that this dry berry husk from the prickly ash tree would bring disease to U.S. citrus trees.

1  The night before you plan on eating these dump-lings, place the soybeans in a large bowl and cover with cold water by 2 inches (5 cm). Soak overnight, then drain well.

2  Transfer the soybeans to a large saucepan and add enough cold water to cover by 1 inch (2.5 cm). Bring to a boil over high heat, then reduce the heat to maintain a steady simmer. Simmer until tender, about 30 minutes. Drain the beans well and cool completely.

3  Meanwhile, bring a small saucepan of salted wa-ter to a boil. Add the bean sprouts and cook until crisp-tender, about 1 minute. Drain, rinse under cold water to stop the cooking, and drain again. Transfer to a food processor and pulse until finely chopped. Transfer the chopped sprouts to a large bowl.

4  In the same food processor (no need to wash it), pulse the tofu until completely broken up. Transfer to the bowl with the bean sprouts, along with the chicken, scallions, bean sauce, chili sauce, pickles, egg yolk, garlic, sesame oil, ginger, pepper, cornstarch, and soybeans.

5  Use your hands to work all the ingredients together until well-mixed. It's best to use your hands because you can get everything incorpo-rated into the meat without making the pieces of meat too small.

6  If you have time, cover and refrigerate the filling until nice and cold, up to 2 days. The filling will be easier to spoon into your wrappers when it's chilled.

7  When you're ready to cook, follow the wrapping and frying instructions on pages 22 to 31.

NOTE: I prefer the Kun Chun brand for both the Chinese bean sauce and Szechuan chili sauce. As for the pickles, I like the Szechuan Food Products brand. All are available at Asian markets and online.

In 2008, my dumpling company raised more than $8,000 for victims of the Szechuan province earthquake by selling these dumplings.

You gotta pour on that extra curry sauce and pour it on *THICK!*

# JAPANESE CURRY CHICKEN DUMPLINGS

MAKES ABOUT 45 DUMPLINGS

Around the corner from my old apartment in New York City's East Village is Curry-Ya, a cute Japanese fast-casual spot. I'm there all the time, downing bowls of their buttery yellow curry slathered over crunchy chicken cutlets. It's the sauce that makes it. That's why I want it inside my dumpling filling and as a dip too. You can even double the sauce below to have enough to completely drown your dumplings. Maybe that's overkill. Then again, maybe not.

- 3 tablespoons unsalted butter
- ¼ cup (35 g) all-purpose flour
- 1 tablespoon yellow curry powder
- 1 tablespoon garam masala
- 1 tablespoon ketchup
- 1 tablespoon Worcestershire sauce
- ¼ teaspoon freshly ground black pepper
- 8 ounces (225 g) fatty (80/20) ground pork
- 8 ounces (225 g) ground dark-meat chicken
- ½ cup (68 g) frozen peas, thawed
- 2 tablespoons finely chopped onion
- 2 teaspoons minced peeled fresh ginger
- 1 teaspoon kosher salt
- 1 (1-pound/455-g) package round dumpling wrappers

1 Melt the butter in a medium saucepan over medium-low heat. Add the flour and cook, stirring continuously, until browned and the raw smell dissipates, about 2 minutes. Add the curry powder, garam masala, ketchup, Worcestershire sauce, and pepper. Cook, stirring continuously, for 1 minute. Continue stirring while adding 1 cup (240 ml) water. Bring to a boil and simmer, stirring frequently, until the sauce has thickened. Transfer ½ cup (120 ml) to a large bowl and let cool to room temperature. Reserve the remaining sauce in a separate bowl for serving.

2 After the sauce in the bowl has cooled, add the pork, chicken, peas, onion, ginger, and salt. Use your hands to work all the ingredients together until well-mixed. It's best to use your hands because you can get everything incorporated into the meat without making the pieces of meat too small.

3 If you have time, cover and refrigerate the filling until nice and cold, up to 2 days. The filling will be easier to spoon into your wrappers when it's chilled.

4 When you're ready to cook, follow the wrapping and frying instructions on pages 22 to 31. Serve the dumplings with the reserved dipping sauce, reheating if needed.

# CHICKEN *SAAG* DUMPLINGS

MAKES ABOUT 45 DUMPLINGS

When I eat Indian food, I like to have all my dishes run into each other on the plate. Once my spinach *saag* starts spilling into my tandoori chicken, I swipe the two together with a warm piece of naan bread. Here I've transformed that mouthful into a spiced filling enriched with coconut milk.

2 pounds (910 g) spinach leaves, washed well
1 pound (455 g) ground dark-meat chicken
¼ cup (60 ml) coconut milk

1 tablespoon garam masala
2 teaspoons minced peeled fresh ginger
2 teaspoons finely chopped scallions, white parts only

1 teaspoon kosher salt
1 (1-pound/455-g) package round dumpling wrappers
Lemon-Yogurt Dip (page 112)

1  Fill a large saucepan with 1 inch (2.5 cm) water. Bring to a boil and add the spinach leaves. Stir well, cover, and steam until just tender and bright green, about 1 minute. Drain immediately. When cool enough to handle, squeeze as much liquid as possible out of the spinach leaves.

2  Chop the spinach and transfer to a large bowl. Add the chicken, coconut milk, garam masala, ginger, scallions, and salt. Use your hands to work all the ingredients together until well-mixed. It's best to use your hands because you can get everything incorporated into the meat without making the pieces of meat too small.

3  If you have time, cover and refrigerate the filling until nice and cold, up to 2 days. The filling will be easier to spoon into your wrappers when it's chilled.

4  When you're ready to cook, follow the wrapping and frying instructions on pages 22 to 31. Serve the dumplings with the Lemon-Yogurt Dip.

Zen out
with a
dumpling-
making
session.

# HERBY TURKEY DUMPLINGS

MAKES ABOUT 45 DUMPLINGS

I'm all about going green. Here, I pack tons of leafy herbs into the filling, then use even more for the creamy dipping sauce. The big blast of freshness stays earthy with dark-meat turkey, which tastes rich and gamey without being too assertive.

1 pound (455 g) ground dark-meat turkey

2 cups (50 g) packed fresh basil leaves, finely chopped

2 cups (50 g) packed fresh cilantro with stems, finely chopped

1 cup (100 g) finely chopped scallions

4 teaspoons fish sauce

Zest and juice of 2 limes

2 teaspoons packed brown sugar

1 (1-pound/455-g) package round dumpling wrappers

New Green Goddess Dip (page 113)

1  In a large bowl, combine the turkey, basil, cilantro, scallions, fish sauce, lime zest and juice, and brown sugar. Use your hands to work all the ingredients together until well-mixed. It's best to use your hands because you can get everything incorporated into the meat without making the pieces of meat too small.

2  If you have time, cover and refrigerate the filling until nice and cold, up to 2 days. The filling will be easier to spoon into your wrappers when it's chilled.

3  When you're ready to cook, follow the wrapping and frying instructions on pages 22 to 31. Serve the dumplings with the New Green Goddess Dip.

If I had to divvy up my dumplings into daytime or nighttime food, I'd definitely put this fresh and bright one in the daytime category.

GREEN GODDESS
is making a
comeback.

# PEKING DUCK DUMPLINGS

MAKES ABOUT 45 DUMPLINGS

Holy smoke! That's all I have to say about this one. What I love is that this takes a super-classic Chinese dish and stuffs it into a dumpling. When fried nice and brown, these dumplings really give you the whole Peking duck experience, as if you're eating the crisp skin and all. When chef Anita Lo first made these dumplings for Rickshaw and gave me one to taste, I felt like I understood the awesomeness of duck for the first time. Some people are kinda wary of duck because it tends to be gamey, but that's what makes it so great. It tastes like animal. You know, real meat—a tender, juicy, naughty morsel.

12 ounces (340 g) Napa cabbage, cored and finely chopped
2¼ teaspoons kosher salt
1 pound (455 g) ground duck
⅓ cup (35 g) finely chopped scallions

1 large egg, beaten
3 tablespoons hoisin
1 tablespoon soy sauce
2 teaspoons cornstarch
1 teaspoon Chinese five-spice powder

1 teaspoon freshly ground black pepper
1 (1-pound/455-g) package round dumpling wrappers
Hoisin Dip (page 108)

If you have a meat grinder and duck dark meat and fat, you want to do a 6 to 1 ratio of meat to fat. Otherwise, find a butcher who does ground duck or try this with dark-meat turkey. It's the closest thing to gamey duck. Better yet, try the Chinatown variation, on the opposite page.

We're bringing *SEXY QUACK* with this one!

1   In a fine-mesh colander, mix the cabbage and 2 teaspoons salt. Let stand while you get everything else ready, at least 10 minutes. Grab handfuls of the cabbage and squeeze as hard as you can to get rid of all the liquid.

2   Transfer the dried cabbage to a large bowl and add the duck, scallions, egg, hoisin, soy sauce, cornstarch, five-spice powder, pepper, and remaining ¼ teaspoon salt. Use your hands to work all the ingredients together until well-mixed. It's best to use your hands because you can get everything incorporated into the meat without making the pieces of meat too small.

3   If you have time, cover and refrigerate the filling until nice and cold, up to 2 days. The filling will be easier to spoon into your wrappers when it's chilled.

4   When you're ready to cook, follow the wrapping and frying instructions on pages 22 to 31. Serve the dumplings with the Hoisin Dip.

## CHINATOWN
## PEKING DUCK DUMPLINGS

Start by taking a trip to Chinatown and buying a whole Peking duck. Remove the skin. Pull the duck meat from the bones by shredding it off with a fork. Chop about one-third of the skin and meat (1 pound/455 g) for the filling. (Snack on the rest!) Omit the soy sauce, cornstarch, and five-spice powder.

Use the
Half-Moon Fold!

Old-school
chowder meets
Thai beach food
in this one!

# LOBSTER WONTONS IN CORN CHOWDER

SERVES 8 TO 12

In the summer, there's nothing like corn and lobster together. With this dumpling soup, you get all of the heartiness of a chowder with light seafood and sweet corn. I like to add fresh kernels at the end for an al dente crunch in the creamy blended soup. And the lobster highlights those fresh, seasonal flavors. Because this shellfish tastes so special on its own, it gets nothing more than lemon and salt. This combo may sound fancy pants, but it's actually a super-casual party dish. It'd be perfect for a weekend at the beach.

**FOR THE CORN CHOWDER:**
5 large ears corn
1 medium onion, chopped
½ lemongrass stalk, chopped
½ head garlic, cut in half crosswise
1 (15-ounce/430-g) can coconut milk

1 cup (140 g) diced peeled all-purpose potato
1 tablespoon curry powder
Kosher salt
Freshly ground black pepper

**FOR THE LOBSTER WONTONS:**
12 ounces (340 g) cooked lobster meat, finely chopped

2 teaspoons fresh lemon juice
Kosher salt
24 round dumpling or wonton wrappers
Cilantro leaves, for garnish
Thinly sliced scallions, for garnish
Lime wedges, for serving

1 **Make the corn chowder:** Cut the kernels off the corn cobs and reserve. You should have about 5 cups (725 g). Place the cobs in a large saucepot and add the onion, lemongrass, garlic, and 2 quarts (2 L) water. Bring to a boil over high heat, then reduce the heat to maintain a simmer for 1 hour. Strain the corn broth through a sieve into a large saucepan; discard the solids.

2 Stir in the coconut milk, potato, curry powder, and half of the corn kernels. Bring the chowder to a boil over high heat, then reduce the heat to medium and simmer until the potatoes are tender, about 10 minutes. Use a stand or immersion blender to puree the soup until very smooth. Season to taste with salt and pepper. Keep warm over low heat.

3 **Make the wontons:** In a large bowl, toss the lobster with the lemon juice and season with salt. Divide the filling among the dumpling wrappers, placing the filling in the center. With a wet fingertip, moisten the entire edge of 1 wrapper and fold in half. Press the edges to seal, squeezing out any air between the filling and wrappers. Repeat with the remaining wrappers.

4 Bring the soup back to a boil. Add the wontons and remaining corn and cook until the dumpling skins are cooked through and the corn is al dente, about 5 minutes.

5 Garnish with the cilantro and scallions. Serve with lime wedges.

# SHRIMP NORI DUMPLINGS

MAKES ABOUT 45 DUMPLINGS

In dim sum restaurants, one of my favorite dumplings is the *har gow*. They're basically huge hunks of shrimp in chewy crystal-clear wrappers. The traditional wrappers are made with tapioca starch and wheat starch—ingredients that are hard to find and even harder to manipulate into sticky yet supple wrappers. I found that this shrimpy mix—with sea-salty roasted seaweed, crunchy jicama, and a spicy sweet sauce—tastes just as good in regular wrappers.

1 pound (455 g) extra-large (26/30-count) shrimp, peeled and deveined
1½ tablespoons sugar
1½ tablespoons oyster sauce
1 tablespoon *aonori* flakes (see Note)
1 large egg white

2½ teaspoons potato starch
2½ teaspoons fresh lemon juice
1¼ teaspoons soy sauce
1¼ teaspoons sriracha
1½ teaspoons kosher salt
¾ cup (90 g) finely diced peeled jicama

½ cup (50 g) thinly sliced scallions
1 (1-pound/455-g) package round dumpling wrappers
Creamy Wasabi Dip (page 110)

1 Cut one-quarter of the shrimp into ¼-inch (6-mm) pieces. Place the remaining three-quarters shrimp in a food processor and add the sugar, oyster sauce, *aonori* flakes, egg white, potato starch, lemon juice, soy sauce, sriracha, and salt. Pulse until well-combined, but not pureed. Transfer to a large bowl and add the jicama, scallions, and chopped shrimp. Use your hands to work all the ingredients together until well-mixed.

2 If you have time, cover and refrigerate the filling until nice and cold, up to 2 days. The filling will be easier to spoon into your wrappers when it's chilled.

3 When you're ready to cook, follow the wrapping and frying instructions on pages 22 to 31. Serve the dumplings with the Creamy Wasabi Dip.

NOTE: *Aonori* flakes are basically thinly sliced roasted seaweed. If you can't find them, you can buy packs of roasted salted seaweed and slice them up yourself.

# NORI SCHOOL

---

## HOW DOES FRESH SEAWEED GO FROM SLIMY VEG TO CRISP SHEETS OF DELECTABLE DRIED NORI?

---

1. Fresh seaweed is chopped up.

2. The chopped seaweed is mixed with water into a slurry.

3. The seaweed slurry is poured onto a wood-framed mat to let excess water drip out and off. This is the hard part!

4. The frame is then lifted off and propped on its side to let the seaweed sheet dry.

   Not exactly a DIY sorta thing. Leave this one to the pros.

MAKES
ABOUT 45
DUMPLINGS

Make Peas
(Dumplings),
Not War!

# PEA SHOOTS & LEEK DUMPLINGS

Pea shoots sound so fancy, but they're really just the greens on pea plants. And they're super tasty, with the grassy edge of leafy greens and the sweetness of peas all rolled into one. They're not as floppy as other greens when cooked, either. They keep their snap, which you can really taste in these springtime dumplings.

1¼ pounds (570 g) pea shoots, trimmed
3 cups (105 g) dried shiitake mushrooms
Boiling water, as needed
1 tablespoon plus 1 teaspoon canola oil
3 cups (270 g) diced leeks, white and pale green parts only

Kosher salt and freshly ground black pepper
6 ounces (170 g) extra-firm tofu
1 large egg white
1½ cups (202 g) frozen peas, thawed
¼ cup (60 ml) oyster sauce

2 teaspoons sugar
1 teaspoon minced garlic
¼ teaspoon minced peeled fresh ginger
1 (1-pound/455-g) package dumpling wrappers
*Mimi* Dip (page 105)

1   Bring a large saucepan of salted water to a boil. Fill a large bowl with ice and water. Plunge the pea shoots into the boiling water and cook until bright green and crisp-tender, about 2 minutes. Drain and immediately transfer to the ice water. Drain well and squeeze out any excess liquid.

2   Meanwhile, place the mushrooms in a medium heatproof bowl and cover with boiling water. Let stand until softened, about 40 minutes. Drain well, trim off and discard the stems, and squeeze out any excess liquid from the caps.

3   In a large skillet, heat 1 teaspoon oil over medium heat. Add the leeks, season with salt and pepper, and cook, stirring occasionally, until tender but not browned, about 5 minutes. Remove from the heat and let cool completely.

4   Place the pea shoots in a food processor and pulse until chopped, with no pieces larger than 1 inch (2.5 cm). Transfer to a large bowl. Place the mushrooms in the processor (no need to clean it) and pulse until finely chopped. Add to the pea shoots. Place the tofu and egg white in the processor (again, no washing!), and process until very smooth. Add to the bowl, along with the leeks, peas, oyster sauce, sugar, garlic, ginger, and ½ teaspoon each salt and pepper.

5   Stir the filling well with a rubber spatula until evenly mixed.

6   When you're ready to cook, follow the wrapping and frying instructions on pages 22 to 31. Serve the dumplings with the *Mimi* Dip.

# EDAMAME DUMPLINGS

MAKES ABOUT 45 DUMPLINGS

For a super fast, super tasty filling, you can't go wrong with these vegan green dumplings. They're my go-to recipe for the cooking classes I teach because the filling is so simple to wrap. The best part is that you can totally adjust all the seasonings to taste because all the ingredients can be safely eaten uncooked.

3 tablespoons extra-virgin olive oil

2 tablespoons soy sauce

¼ teaspoon crushed red chile flakes

1 pound (455 g) frozen shelled edamame, thawed

2 lemons

Kosher salt and freshly ground black pepper

1 (1-pound/455-g) package round dumpling wrappers

Lemon Sansho Dip (page 111)

1　In a food processor, combine the oil, soy sauce, chile flakes, and two-thirds of the edamame and puree until smooth. Add the remaining edamame and pulse just until coarsely chopped.

2　Transfer the mixture to a large bowl and zest the lemons directly into the mixture, then squeeze in the juice of 1 lemon. Stir well with a rubber spatula until evenly mixed. Taste and season with salt, pepper, and more lemon juice.

3　When you're ready to cook, follow the wrapping and frying instructions on pages 22 to 31. Serve the dumplings with the Lemon Sansho Dip.

This is the vegetarian dumpling for omnivores. It is so hearty and tasty that you will have even the biggest meat-eaters begging for more of these.

# MINTY SNOW PEA DUMPLINGS

MAKES ABOUT 50 DUMPLINGS

When I first tried making these, I kept wanting more mintiness. Not toothpaste-intense, just a little more brightness with the sweet peas. Turns out all I had to do was keep the tender stems on the mint. I got to save a step in prepping while amping up the flavor. That's totally my kind of cooking.

10 ounces (280 g) firm tofu
2 tablespoons sugar
2 teaspoons canola oil
2 cups (270 g) frozen peas, thawed
3 cups (280 g) fresh snow peas, strings removed and very thinly sliced at an angle

1 cup (25 g) packed fresh mint with tender stems, very finely chopped
2 tablespoons finely chopped scallions
1 tablespoon fresh lemon juice

1 tablespoon kosher salt
2 teaspoons minced peeled fresh ginger
1 teaspoon freshly ground black pepper
1 (1-pound/455-g) package round dumpling wrappers
Lemon Sansho Dip (page 111)

1   In a food processor, combine the tofu, sugar, and oil and puree until smooth. Add 1 cup (135 g) peas and pulse until almost smooth.

2   Transfer the mixture to a large bowl and add the snow peas, mint, scallions, lemon juice, salt, ginger, pepper, and remaining 1 cup (135 g) peas. Stir well with a rubber spatula until evenly mixed.

3   When you're ready to cook, follow the wrapping and frying instructions on pages 22 to 31. Serve the dumplings with the Lemon Sansho Dip.

Sparkly mint plus sweet peas equals HAPPY MOUTH.

# MUSTARD GREENS & MUSTARD SEED DUMPLINGS

MAKES ABOUT 45 DUMPLINGS

Mustard alone isn't actually spicy, but it's got a great kick. When you pair the pop of the seeds with the bite of mustard greens, you get a hit of earthy heat. Chef Anita Lo, who created these for Rickshaw, killed it with these hearty winter vegetable dumplings!

Kosher salt
1 pound (455 g) mustard greens, tough stems and ribs removed
1½ teaspoons canola oil
1 large egg

3 tablespoons thinly sliced scallions
1½ tablespoons oyster sauce
1¼ teaspoons yellow mustard seeds
½ teaspoon minced garlic

½ teaspoon dry mustard powder mixed with ½ teaspoon water
Freshly ground black pepper
1 (1-pound/455-g) package round dumpling wrappers
Toasted Sesame–Soy Dip (page 103)

1   Bring a large saucepan of salted water to a boil. Fill a large bowl with ice and water. Plunge the mustard greens into the boiling water and cook until bright green and crisp-tender, about 5 minutes. Drain and immediately transfer to the ice water. Drain well and squeeze out any excess liquid.

2   In a small skillet, heat ½ teaspoon oil over medium heat. Break the egg into the skillet and season with salt. Use a rubber spatula to break the yolk, then let sit while the whites sizzle. As soon as the whites are almost set, stir the egg while tilting the pan to hassle them a little. You don't want the eggs fluffy, but they should still be a little wet. Transfer the runny egg to a large bowl.

3   Place the mustard greens in a food processor and pulse until finely chopped but not pureed. Transfer to the bowl with the egg, along with the scallions, oyster sauce, mustard seeds, garlic,

mustard powder mixture, remaining 1 teaspoon oil, and ½ teaspoon each salt and pepper. Stir well with a rubber spatula until evenly mixed.

4   When you're ready to cook, follow the wrapping and frying instructions on pages 22 to 31. Serve the dumplings with the Toasted Sesame–Soy Dip.

# HASSLED EGGS & KALE DUMPLINGS

MAKES ABOUT 45 DUMPLINGS

Kale salad (see page 145) may be all the rage, but the greens are great in dumplings, too. To stuff the shredded leaves into the wrappers raw, I bind them with scrambled eggs. The technique was inspired by a Northern Chinese dish called *jiu cai he zi*. The original encases a large, round chive omelet in a fried flour dough. My dumplings taste like the mini version of that pie.

1 teaspoon canola oil
4 large eggs
½ teaspoon kosher salt
8 ounces (225 g) Chinese-spiced thick dry tofu or extra-firm tofu, finely diced

1 cup (20 g) packed very finely chopped fresh kale leaves
2 tablespoons minced Chinese garlic chives
1 tablespoon minced onion
1 tablespoon *Nori Furikake* (see page 158) or store-bought

½ teaspoon soy sauce
½ teaspoon sesame oil
½ teaspoon sugar
1 (1-pound/455-g) package round dumpling wrappers
Vinegar-Ginger Dip (page 102)

If you have leftover dumplings from dinner, crisp 'em up in a hot skillet for breakfast. They're great with a hot cup of coffee.

1   Heat the oil in a large nonstick skillet over medium heat. Break three eggs into the skillet and season with ¼ teaspoon salt. Use a rubber spatula to break the yolks, then let sit while the whites sizzle. As soon as the whites are almost set, stir the eggs while tilting the pan to hassle them a little. You don't want the eggs fluffy, but they should still be a little wet. Transfer the runny eggs to a large bowl.

2   Add the tofu, kale, chives, onion, *nori furikake*, soy sauce, sesame oil, sugar, and remaining ¼ teaspoon salt to the bowl. Stir with a spatula until well-mixed. Let cool to room temperature. Break the remaining egg into the mixture and stir until incorporated.

3   When you're ready to cook, follow the wrapping and frying instructions on pages 22 to 31. Serve the dumplings with the Vinegar-Ginger Dip.

# MUSHROOM DUMPLINGS

MAKES ABOUT 45 DUMPLINGS

When I began experimenting with re-creating hot and sour soup in dumpling form, I couldn't quite nail the sour part. Then I realized all I had to do was dunk the finished dumpling in my vinegar dip. Lots of mushrooms give the peppery filling umami, and a swish in the sauce delivers a tangy finish. Nailed it!

4 teaspoons canola oil
½ cup (60 g) minced onion
1 teaspoon kosher salt
8 ounces (225 g) fresh
   shiitake mushroom caps,
   very thinly sliced
2 tablespoons Shaoxing wine

2 pounds (910 g) white
   button mushrooms, trimmed
   and finely diced
⅔ cup (165 g) finely diced
   extra-firm tofu, preferably
   Chinese pressed brown tofu

⅓ cup (16 g) finely chopped
   Chinese garlic chives
2 teaspoons soy sauce
½ teaspoon freshly ground
   black pepper
Vinegar-Ginger Dip (page 102)

1   Heat 2 teaspoons oil in a large skillet over medium-high heat. Add ¼ cup (30 g) onion and ¼ teaspoon salt. Cook, stirring occasionally, until the onion is just sizzling, about 1 minute. Add the shiitakes and cook, stirring occasionally, for 2 minutes. Add 1 tablespoon wine and cook until it is evaporated. Continue cooking until the mushrooms are lightly browned. Transfer to a large bowl.

2   Repeat with the remaining 2 teaspoons oil, ¼ cup (30 g) onion, ¼ teaspoon salt, the button mushrooms, and 1 tablespoon wine. Transfer to the bowl with the shiitakes. Stir in the tofu, garlic chives, soy sauce, pepper, and remaining ½ teaspoon salt. Let the filling cool to room temperature.

3   When you're ready to cook, follow the wrapping and frying instructions on pages 22 to 31. Serve the dumplings with the Vinegar-Ginger Dip.

# DUMPLINGS BY THE NUMBERS

## 220

Number of dumplings
a pro can wrap in an hour

That's 3
or 4 a minute,
guys. Put away
those phones
and GET
CRACKIN'!

(For the
THIN
ONES.)

## 50

Number of skins in
my favorite pack of
dumpling wrappers

## 9

Number of
dumplings for
a full meal

When I say 9,
I REALLY
MEAN 12.

## 4

Number of times
I have steamed
dumplings at home
instead of frying

## 3

Number of times
I said I could be
vegetarian after
eating edamame
dumplings

# BUTTERNUT SQUASH–CORN DUMPLINGS

This little dumpling gives butternut squash soup a run for its money.

MAKES ABOUT 45 DUMPLINGS

The end of summer's the best for these. Corn (straight from the farm, please!) tastes so sweet, and the first squash of the season is more sugary than starchy. To cut through the double dose of sweetness, I combine the heat of fresh ginger with cayenne.

½ butternut squash (1 pound/ 455 g), peeled, seeded and cut into chunks
2 teaspoons dark brown sugar
2 teaspoons minced onion

1 teaspoon minced peeled fresh ginger
½ teaspoon coconut oil
½ teaspoon kosher salt
⅛ teaspoon cayenne pepper

1 cup (145 g) fresh corn kernels
1 (1-pound/455-g) package round dumpling wrappers
Lemon Sansho Dip (page 111)

1   Prepare a steamer. Steam the squash until tender, about 20 minutes. A thin paring knife should be able to slide through the squash easily.

2   Transfer the squash to a large bowl and add the brown sugar, onion, ginger, coconut oil, salt, and cayenne. Mash it with a fork until almost completely smooth. Stir in the corn until it's evenly distributed. Let the filling cool to room temperature.

3   When you're ready to cook, follow the wrapping and frying instructions on pages 22 to 31. Serve the dumplings with the Lemon Sansho Dip.

# SMASHED SWEET POTATO DUMPLINGS

MAKES ABOUT 45 DUMPLINGS

In the dead of winter, I crave food with color. Sweet potatoes totally rock on gray days. And they're yummy enough to elevate frozen corn when fresh isn't available. The corn adds bits of texture, as do the potatoes themselves. Don't go crazy mashing them. You're not going for baby food here—you want them just cohesive enough to wrap.

1 pound (455 g) sweet potatoes, peeled and cut into
   1-inch (2.5-cm) chunks
2 tablespoons unsalted butter
1¼ teaspoons sugar

1¼ teaspoons kosher salt
1¼ teaspoons freshly ground
   black pepper
1 cup (145 g) frozen corn
   kernels, thawed

1 (1-pound/455-g) package
   round dumpling wrappers
Lemon Sansho Dip (page 111)

1   Prepare a steamer. Steam the sweet potatoes until
    tender but not mushy, about 15 minutes. A thin paring
    knife should be able to slide through the sweet pota-
    toes easily.

2   Transfer the sweet potatoes to a large bowl and add the
    butter, sugar, salt, and pepper. Mash with a fork until
    just combined. You want to keep plenty of chunks in
    there. Stir in the corn until it's evenly distributed. Let
    the filling cool to room temperature.

3   When you're ready to cook, follow the wrapping and
    frying instructions on pages 22 to 31. Serve the dump-
    lings with the Lemon Sansho Dip.

I met my husband, John,
in front of the first
Rickshaw restaurant on 23rd
Street. He's vegetarian and
came up with this delightful
recipe, which ended up being
a smash hit.

# CHICKPEA DUMPLINGS

MAKES ABOUT 45 DUMPLINGS

My Asian take on hummus hints at the sesame flavor of tahini with the combo of sesame oil and hoisin sauce. Because I don't actually want the texture of a dip as my filling, I throw in my favorite colorful crunchy veggies.

2 (15.5-ounce/445-g) cans chickpeas, rinsed and drained
4 teaspoons canola oil
2 teaspoons sesame oil
1 cup (150 g) finely diced red bell pepper

½ cup (65 g) finely diced carrot
¼ cup (30 g) finely diced red onion
¼ cup (60 ml) hoisin
2 tablespoons fresh lemon juice

2 teaspoons soy sauce
1½ teaspoons kosher salt
1 (1-pound/455-g) package round dumpling wrappers
Lemon-Yogurt Dip (page 112)

1  In a food processor, combine half of the chickpeas with the canola oil and sesame oil. Pulse until smooth.

2  Transfer to a large bowl and add the bell pepper, carrot, onion, hoisin, lemon juice, soy sauce, salt, and the remaining chickpeas. Stir with a spatula until well-mixed.

3  When you're ready to cook, follow the wrapping and frying instructions on pages 22 to 31. Serve the dumplings with the Lemon-Yogurt Dip.

Sometimes, I enjoy spoonfuls of this savory filling the way other people do raw cookie dough. In this case, it's totally safe to eat uncooked!

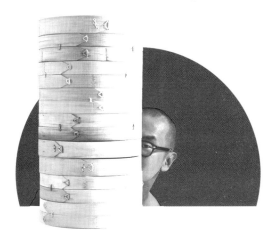

# LENTIL-SPINACH *MOMOS*

MAKES ABOUT 45 DUMPLINGS

Traditionally, *momos* have fillings that range from lamb to lentils in thick, bready wrappers. I prefer using thinner wrappers while keeping the stuffing hearty enough for winter meals. To enrich nubby lentils, I mix them with my take on *saag*-inspired creamed spinach.

⅓ cup (65 g) French Le Puy
  lentils, picked over and
  rinsed well
Cold water, as needed
Kosher salt
1 pound (455 g) spinach,
  washed well

¼ cup (35 ml) extra-virgin
  olive oil
¼ cup (36 g) all-purpose flour
1 tablespoon ground cumin
1 cup (225 g) full-fat
  cottage cheese
1 teaspoon fresh lemon juice

Freshly ground black pepper
1 (1-pound/455-g) package
  round dumpling wrappers
Lemon-Yogurt Dip (page 112)
Scallions, thinly sliced, for
  garnish

1   In a medium saucepan, cover the lentils with cold water by 1 inch (2.5 cm). Bring to a boil, then reduce the heat to simmer the lentils until tender, about 17 minutes. Drain well. You should have 1 cup (155 g) cooked lentils.

2   Meanwhile, bring a large saucepan of salted water to a boil. Fill a large bowl with ice and water. Plunge the spinach into the boiling water and cook until bright green and wilted, about 30 seconds. Drain and immediately transfer to the ice water. Drain well and squeeze out any excess liquid. Coarsely chop the spinach. You should have 2 cups (480 g) chopped spinach.

3   In the same large saucepan, heat the oil over medium-low heat. Stir in the flour and continue stirring until the mixture browns a bit. Whisk in the cumin, then the cottage cheese and spinach. Stir until well-combined. Remove the pan from the heat and stir in the lentils and lemon juice. Season with salt and pepper to taste. Let cool to room temperature.

4   When you're ready to cook, follow the wrapping and frying instructions on pages 22 to 31. Serve the dumplings with the Lemon-Yogurt Dip, topped with the scallions.

For a heartier take, wrap these in the Wheat Flour Wrappers (page 47).

I love Tibetan *momos*—starting with their name!

# INDIAN STREET-MARKET DUMPLINGS

These wrapper-less lentil dumplings are India's answer to hush puppies. They're crisp and craggy on the outside and fluffy and nutty on the inside. I season mine the way I've tasted them on the side of the road in India, with fresh ginger in the lentil mix and pinches of spice on top. These crunchy bites make the perfect snack and starter, but they're also substantial enough to serve as a great vegetarian main course.

1 cup (190 g) *urad dal* (split and skinned black Indian lentils; see Notes)
Cold water, as needed
1 teaspoon grated peeled fresh ginger

1 teaspoon kosher salt
¼ teaspoon *asafetida* powder (see Notes)
2 cups (480 ml) canola oil
Lemon-Yogurt Dip (page 112)
Ground cumin, for serving
Ground coriander, for serving

Ground dried red chiles, for serving
Chopped fresh cilantro, for serving
Finely diced onion, for serving

1   In a large bowl, cover the *urad dal* with cold water by 1 inch (2.5 cm). Soak at room temperature for 4 hours. Drain and transfer to a food processor, along with the ginger, salt, and *asafetida*. Process, scraping the sides of the bowl occasionally, until fluffy but still chunky. The mixture should hold together when you squeeze it. If it doesn't, add a little water and process again. Transfer to a bowl, press plastic wrap directly on the surface of the mixture, and refrigerate for at least 15 minutes and up to overnight.

2   Spread the mixture on a cutting board into a 1-inch- (2.5-cm-) thick square. Cut the square into 2-inch- (5-cm-) square patties.

3   Heat the oil in a large, deep skillet over medium-high heat until hot but not smoking. Use a thin offset spatula to slide a square into the hot oil. It should sizzle immediately. If not, remove and wait for the oil to get hotter. Add as many squares as can fit comfortably in the pan without crowding. Fry, turning once, until golden brown. Drain on paper towels. Repeat with the remaining squares.

4   Top the dumplings with the Lemon-Yogurt Dip and sprinkle with cumin, coriander, chiles, cilantro, and onion. Serve immediately.

NOTES: *Urad dal* are Indian black lentils, which look white when sold split and skinned. You can't substitute French Le Puy lentils here because that variety holds its shape when cooked; *urad dal* break down into a puree.

*Asafetida* powder, also known as *hing* in Hindi, is a spice derived from a variety of fennel. You can find it online or in specialty or Indian markets. If you can't find it, substitute a pinch each of onion powder and granulated garlic.

# STREET FOOD

The Silk Road wasn't the only thoroughfare where dumplings were popular. They're currently sold on side streets all over China. And they're in good company: There are so many other foods that originated from street vendors and taste best when eaten on the side of the road! Here are some of my faves.

### INDONESIA BAKSO
This meatball soup, served in a clear broth with noodles, eggs, and shallots, is an Indonesian national favorite.

### TURKEY SIMIT
Imagine a pretzel and a bagel tangled up in a cage fight. The result would be this awesome bread. It's great paired with mint tea in the morning.

### KOREA GIMBAP
Korea's take on sushi. Nori and rice envelop a filling containing anything from crab to pickled vegetables to beef.

### EGYPT TA'AMIYA
This fava bean–based falafel is best when served hot in a pita with crunchy pickled vegetables on top.

### SINGAPORE CHILI CRAB
This steaming plate of seafoody goodness, spiked with hot sauce and fresh herbs, makes for some spicy, messy eating.

### SINGAPORE HAINANESE CHICKEN RICE
Most countries have a chicken and rice dish and this one is especially tasty. The rice is cooked with pandan, a fragrant herb, and the accompanying soy-chile dip is perfect.

### COLOMBIA AREPAS
These crispy corn cakes (think pan-fried polenta with cheese) bring the house down.

### PHILIPPINES HALO-HALO
Affectionately called *halo-halo* (which translates to "mix-mix") in the Philippines, this sticky-sweet mountain of ice cream, shaved ice, red beans, toasted coconut, and evaporated milk is irresistible.

### POLAND PIEROGI
The Polish answer to Chinese dumplings: thick dough wrappers filled with meats and cheeses and fried in butter! What?!

### VIETNAM BANH MI
One of the few good things to come from colonialism is this Southeast Asian take on a sandwich. Take a French baguette and fill it with tasty meat, cucumbers, cilantro, and pickled daikon and you've got yourself a winner.

### TAIWAN FRIED MILK
Condensed milk is mixed into a batter, formed into cubes, and deep-fried. The result is a crispy outer layer that gives way to a center of chewy, creamy sweetness. Oh yeah, and it comes on a stick. The Taiwanese take on a toasted marshmallow!

### MALAYSIA LAKSA
These soup noodles combine the tartness of tamarind with the creaminess of coconut milk. Then the whole mix gets a blast of spice. It's pretty messy, so you'd better check out how to slurp noodle soup on page 133.

### GERMANY CURRYWURST
Fresh porky sausage smothered in a ketchupy, curry-spiced gravy makes me say *mehr bitte*!

### JAPAN TAKOYAKI
Octopus, scallions, and ginger coated in pancake batter are cooked into perfect little balls. I can think of eight great reasons to love this.

### FRANCE SOCCA
This specialty of Nice is a chickpea pancake that is so light and delicious—and gluten-free.

MAKES
ABOUT 24
DUMPLINGS

# PEARL DUMPLINGS

A dim sum classic, these "dumplings" are encased in sticky rice grains instead of classic wrappers. It's such a cool process because all you have to do is coat meatballs with uncooked rice. As they steam, the rice becomes the wrapper. **What the what?!** Traditionally, they're called "pearls" because the rice is all shiny and white. I season my rice with soy sauce and sesame oil to make the whole thing tastier. Yum is right.

1 cup (185 g) uncooked sweet rice (see Note)
Cold water, as needed
1 pound (455 g) fatty (80/20) ground pork
2 large eggs, beaten

2 tablespoons plus ½ teaspoon soy sauce
2 tablespoons finely chopped canned water chestnuts
2¼ teaspoons sesame oil
2 teaspoons sugar
2 teaspoons cornstarch

2 teaspoons Shaoxing wine
2 teaspoons minced peeled fresh ginger
Napa cabbage leaves, for steaming
Vinegar-Ginger Dip (page 102)

**1** Place the rice in a large bowl and cover it with 2 inches (5 cm) cold water. Soak at room temperature for at least 2 hours or up to overnight.

**2** Meanwhile, in a large bowl, combine the pork, eggs, 2 tablespoons soy sauce, water chestnuts, 2 teaspoons sesame oil, sugar, cornstarch, wine, and ginger. Use your hands to work all the ingredients together until well-mixed. It's best to use your hands because you can get everything incorporated into the meat without making the pieces of meat too small.

**3** Freeze the mixture until just firm, about 30 minutes.

**4** Drain the rice well and transfer to a large bowl. Stir in the remaining ½ teaspoon soy sauce and ¼ teaspoon sesame oil.

**5** Dampen your hands and roll heaping tablespoonfuls of the pork mixture into balls. Roll each meatball in the rice mixture to evenly coat it, gently pressing in the rice to stick. Freeze the balls again if they get too soft.

**6** Line a bamboo steamer, steamer basket, or steamer insert with the cabbage leaves. Bring a few inches (5 cm) of water to a steady simmer in a wok or saucepan. Place the balls in the steamer, spacing them 1 inch (2.5 cm) apart. Steam until the rice is tender and the meat is just cooked through, about 15 minutes.

**7** Serve the dumplings hot with the Vinegar-Ginger Dip.

NOTE: Sweet rice, a short-grain variety that becomes very tender and chewy when cooked, is available at Asian markets.

When the kernels of raw rice turn into a sticky rice dumpling wrapper, it's like *MAGIC!*

# CHAPTER 2

# DIPS

Just because dips go on last doesn't mean they aren't the best—and arguably most important—part of the dumpling experience. Typically, dips are very basic and easy to make. They infuse your dumplings with a final hit of bright, fresh flavor. I've offered suggestions for my favorite pairings in this chapter (see chart, page 114), but you should totally experiment and see what you like best. And when you make the dips, experiment with the proportions of the ingredients. The quantities in the recipes that follow are the way I like them, but when you're finished mixing a batch, taste and adjust the seasonings until you're happy. You'll like your own dips so much, you'll want to use them for veggies or chips or crackers. They're also great as salad dressings or sauces, too.

DR. TAN'S
CHILE
DIP

LEMON-
YOGURT
DIP

TOASTED
SESAME–SOY
DIP

CHILE-SOY
DIP

PEANUT
VINAIGRETTE

*MIMI*
DIP

VINEGAR-
GINGER
DIP

NEW
GREEN
GODDESS
DIP

ASIAN
BARBECUE
SAUCE

HOISIN
DIP

# SOY-VINEGAR DIP

The ultimate classic. The proportions below are my ideal, but you should taste and adjust the balance of salty soy to tangy vinegar to your taste. Different brands and styles of soy sauce vary in saltiness, and the same is true of the acidity in rice wine vinegar. Even though this is the most basic sauce, you can go even easier by dipping dumplings in a high-quality soy sauce or vinegar alone.

¼ cup (60 ml) soy sauce
2 tablespoons rice wine
  vinegar
1 garlic clove, smashed
¼ teaspoon freshly ground
  black pepper

In a small bowl, stir together all of the ingredients with 2 tablespoons water. If you have time, cover and refrigerate the mixture overnight. Pick out the garlic and throw it away before serving. The dip can be refrigerated in an airtight container for up to 2 weeks.

# VINEGAR-GINGER DIP

At every soup dumpling joint, servers will drop a dish of pitch-black vinegar with thinly slivered ginger on the table. Chinese black vinegar has an earthy sweetness that offsets the bright heat of fresh ginger. Be sure to use young ginger, which is firm with nearly translucent tissue-thin skin, so you can cut skinny slivers. Older ginger, which has tough wrinkly skin, has a lot of fibers that aren't pleasant to munch on with your dumplings.

½ cup (120 ml) Chinese black
  vinegar
1 teaspoon sugar
2 tablespoons slivered peeled
  fresh ginger

In a small bowl, stir together all of the ingredients with 2 tablespoons water. If you have time, cover and refrigerate the mixture overnight. The dip can be refrigerated in an airtight container for up to 2 weeks.

# TOASTED SESAME–SOY DIP

MAKES ABOUT ½ CUP (120 ML)

A little sesame oil goes a long way. It adds a toasty, nutty richness to a classic soy dip. The key here is to start with good sesame oil. It goes rancid quickly, so make sure you're using a fresh bottle. Do the sniff test. If it smells funky, dump it.

¼ cup (60 ml) soy sauce
2 tablespoons rice wine
  vinegar
1 teaspoon toasted sesame oil
1 garlic clove, smashed
1 teaspoon toasted sesame
  seeds
Pinch freshly ground black
  pepper

In a small bowl, stir together all of the ingredients with 2 tablespoons water. If you have time, cover and refrigerate the mixture overnight. Pick out the garlic and throw it away before serving. The dip can be refrigerated in an airtight container for up to 2 weeks.

# CHILE-SOY DIP

MAKES ABOUT ¾ CUP (180 ML)

Hey hot heads! This one's for you! I love spicy, so I already find this combo pretty intense. If you can handle more, go at it and amp up the heat. The Szechuan chile sauce is made with soybeans, so it has a more rounded flavor, while sriracha is more garlicky and sharp.

½ cup (120 ml) Toasted
  Sesame–Soy Dip (see above)
3 tablespoons Szechuan chile
  sauce (see Note)
1½ tablespoons sriracha

In a small bowl, stir together all of the ingredients. If you have time, cover and refrigerate the mixture overnight. The dip can be refrigerated in an airtight container for up to 2 weeks.

NOTE: Sriracha is everywhere nowadays. You can find Szechuan chile sauce in Asian markets or online.

# DR. TAN'S CHILE DIP

MAKES ABOUT ½ CUP (120 ML)

Dr. Tan lived on my block growing up and was like an uncle to me. His family became my family on dumpling party nights, and his chile dip became one of my favorite foods ever. For our parties, he'd bring over fresh Thai bird chiles that he'd plucked from his garden and make the sauce on the spot. His chiles were so fragrant and fresh, but he didn't use them to hit us over the head with heat. He'd split them to steep in the puckery sweetened vinegar so they'd give the dip lots of flavor and just a touch of heat.

½ cup (120 ml) rice wine
  vinegar
2 tablespoons sugar
1 tablespoon fish sauce
2 small fresh Thai chiles,
  split lengthwise

In a small bowl, stir together all of the ingredients. If you have time, cover and refrigerate the mixture overnight. Pick out and discard the chiles before serving. The dip can be refrigerated in an airtight container for up to 2 weeks.

Working up a sweat while eating chiles ia a great way to stay cool in the summer.

# *MIMI* DIP

MAKES ABOUT ¾ CUP (180 ML)

*Mimi* means "secret" in Chinese. And that's just what this dip was when my Rickshaw restaurant was open. For our staff meals, our cooks Josefat and Juan served this spicy, creamy, dreamy sauce. Once customers got wind of it, they began asking for this off-the-menu sauce. It wasn't long before we made it a regular on the menu.

2 teaspoons sugar
½ cup (120 ml) mayonnaise
2 tablespoons sriracha

In a microwave-safe bowl, heat the sugar with 2 table-spoons water for 30 seconds. Stir well until the sugar dissolves. Let cool to room temperature, then stir in the mayonnaise and sriracha. The dip can be refrigerated in an airtight container for up to 3 days.

Another *mimi* for you: Don't trust anyone who doesn't love mayo.

# SPICY PEANUT DIP

I've seen lots of friends eat this dip straight-up with a spoon. And I'll admit it: I've done it too. Creamy coconut milk brings together sweet peanut butter, spicy chile jam, and funky fish sauce. You can totally double this dip so you can enjoy it long after the dumplings are gone.

2 tablespoons creamy peanut
  butter
2½ teaspoons *nam prik pao*
  (roasted chile jam; see
  Note)
1 tablespoon plus 2 teaspoons
  sugar
1 teaspoon fish sauce
¾ cup (180 ml) coconut milk
Kosher salt and freshly
  ground black pepper

In a small bowl, whisk together the peanut butter, *nam prik pao*, sugar, and fish sauce. Continue whisking and add the coconut milk in a slow, steady stream to emulsify the mixture. Season with salt and pepper to taste. You also can adjust the other seasonings to your taste. The dip can be refrigerated in an airtight container for up to 1 week.

NOTE: *Nam prik pao*, an essential Thai condiment, combines a chile-garlic-shallot paste with funky shrimp paste, fish sauce, sweet palm sugar, and tangy tamarind. It's sometimes labeled roasted chile paste, chile jam, or chile paste in oil. Look for the blend of ingredients above and you've got the right thing.

# PEANUT VINAIGRETTE

MAKES ABOUT ¾ CUP (180 ML)

Sometimes I crave the flavor of peanuts without the thick texture of a dip. Vinegar balances the richness of roasted peanuts here, while cilantro delivers a blast of freshness. I love this on salads and have even put it on grilled meats.

½ cup (72 g) lightly salted dry-roasted peanuts
¼ cup (60 ml) rice wine vinegar
2 tablespoons packed brown sugar

2 tablespoons creamy peanut butter
1 tablespoon finely chopped fresh cilantro

1 tablespoon soy sauce
1½ teaspoons sesame oil
1½ teaspoons minced garlic
½ teaspoon kosher salt

In a food processor or blender, combine the peanuts, vinegar, brown sugar, peanut butter, cilantro, soy sauce, sesame oil, garlic, salt, and ¼ cup (60 ml) water. Puree until smooth. The vinaigrette can be refrigerated in an airtight container for up to 3 days. Shake it well before using.

Keep a jar in your fridge. With a drizzle of this dressing, weekday salads rock!

# HOISIN DIP

MAKES ABOUT ⅔ CUP (165 ML)

Hoisin is the traditional brown sauce you sandwich with Peking duck. With its plummy sweetness, it rounds out the richness of fatty, yummy meat. On its own, hoisin has a pretty intense beany flavor. That's why I like to thin it with water and add the Asian dynamic duo of soy sauce and sesame oil.

1 tablespoon hoisin
2 teaspoons Shaoxing wine
2 teaspoons soy sauce
1 teaspoon sesame oil
¼ teaspoon freshly ground
  black pepper

In a small bowl, whisk together the hoisin, wine, soy sauce, sesame oil, and pepper with ½ cup (120 ml) water until smooth. The dip can be refrigerated in an airtight container for up to 1 week.

# ASIAN BARBECUE SAUCE

MAKES ABOUT 1¼ CUPS (300 ML)

Using dried fruits in a sauce may seem weird, but I puree dried tropical fruits for their unique vibrant sweetness. They're a natural pairing for the sweetness in Chinese hoisin and Korean *gochujang*. Both sauces start with soybeans as their base, which lend an earthy sweetness. I pair those sauces with Mexican jalapeños to make this a melting pot sauce that tastes great with all types of cuisines.

¼ cup (29 g) dried mango
¼ cup (29 g) dried pineapple
Hot water, as needed
¼ cup (50 g) sugar
6 tablespoons (90 ml) red
  wine vinegar

¼ cup (60 ml) ketchup
¼ cup (60 ml) hoisin
¼ cup (60 ml) *gochujang*
  (Korean chile-bean paste)

1 slice pickled jalapeño
  plus 1 tablespoon pickling
  liquid
¼ teaspoon kosher salt

1   Place the mango and pineapple in a heatproof bowl and cover with hot water; let sit until softened, about 10 minutes. Drain and chop.

2   Place the sugar in a small saucepan and cook over medium-low heat until caramelized and dark amber, swirling the pan occasionally to evenly brown. Remove the pan from the heat and stir in the chopped dried fruit. Let cool to room temperature.

3   Transfer the fruit to a food processor or blender along with the vinegar, ketchup, hoisin, *gochujang*, jalapeño with liquid, and salt. Pulse until well-blended but still slightly chunky. The barbecue sauce can be refrigerated in an airtight container for up to 2 weeks.

# CREAMY WASABI DIP

MAKES ABOUT ½ CUP (120 ML)

Tofu tempers the sharpness of wasabi in this dip, which tastes like a marriage of horseradish and hot mustard. I especially love this dip with seafood. White soy keeps the dip a pretty light green color. If you don't care about that, you can sub regular soy.

1 tablespoon wasabi powder
4 ounces (115 g) regular
  tofu, drained

1 tablespoon chopped
  scallions
2 tablespoons white soy sauce

2 teaspoons sugar
Pinch freshly ground black
  pepper

1   In a small bowl, stir the wasabi powder into 2 tablespoons water until smooth and pasty.

2   Puree the tofu in a food processor until smooth. Add the scallions, soy sauce, sugar, pepper, and wasabi paste. Puree until smooth. The dip can be refrigerated in an airtight container for up to 1 day.

Obsessed with protein? Get another dose from this dip!

# LEMON SANSHO DIP

MAKES ABOUT ⅔ CUP (165 ML)

Lemon juice and soy sauce go so well together. Add a hit of Japanese sansho pepper and the already complex combo gets even yummier. Anita Lo created this dip to accompany Rickshaw's superpopular vegetarian Edamame Dumplings (page 81) and it balances the heartiness of that protein-packed fave so well!

¼ cup (60 ml) fresh lemon
   juice
2 tablespoons soy sauce
1 teaspoon ground sansho
   pepper (see Note)
¼ teaspoon freshly ground
   black pepper

In a small bowl, whisk together all of the ingredients with ¼ cup (60 ml) water. If you have time, cover and refrigerate the mixture overnight. The dip can be refrigerated in an airtight container for up to 2 weeks.

NOTE: Sansho is a variety of peppercorn native to Japan. Its multidimensional floral aroma comes with a bit of heat for a well-rounded flavor.

Bright, right, and out of sight!

# LEMON-YOGURT DIP

MAKES ABOUT 1 CUP (240 ML)

Whenever I want a dip to cool a hot, spiced filling, I go for yogurt. Lemon juice elevates the tanginess of plain yogurt and highlights the flavors of assertive dumpling fillings.

1 cup (240 ml) plain whole-
  milk yogurt
2 tablespoons fresh lemon
  juice
Kosher salt and freshly
  ground black pepper

In a small bowl, stir together the yogurt and lemon juice. Season with salt and pepper to taste. The dip can be refrigerated in an airtight container for up to 3 days.

# MINTY GREEN DIP

MAKES ABOUT ¾ CUP (180 ML)

Fresh and beautiful, this dip is loaded with mint, which pairs perfectly with heartier dumplings. I especially love it with the Cumin Lamb (page 61) and Chicken *Saag* Dumplings (page 68). Sometimes, I go all-green and dunk the Herby Turkey Dumplings (page 70) in it!

1¼ cups (30 g) packed fresh
  mint leaves
¼ cup (6 g) packed fresh
  cilantro leaves

2 tablespoons finely chopped
  peeled fresh ginger
¼ teaspoon minced garlic
¼ teaspoon minced fresh green
  chili

¼ teaspoon kosher salt
¼ teaspoon sugar
¼ cup (60 ml) fresh lemon
  juice

In a food processor, combine all of the ingredients with 6 tablespoons water. Process until smooth. Add more water if needed to achieve a runny consistency. The dip can be refrigerated in an airtight container for up to 1 day.

# NEW GREEN GODDESS DIP

Green goddess goes Asian in my take on the classic dressing. Cilantro with stems is key here. You get a more pronounced coriander note that way. Of course, this dip doubles as an easy salad dressing too.

¼ cup (6 g) packed fresh basil leaves, finely chopped

¼ cup (6 g) packed fresh cilantro with stems, finely chopped

¼ cup (60 ml) mayonnaise

2 tablespoons fresh lemon juice

1 tablespoon finely chopped scallions

½ teaspoon kosher salt

Pinch freshly ground black pepper

In a small bowl, stir together the basil, cilantro, mayonnaise, lemon juice, scallions, salt, and pepper until smooth. This dip can be refrigerated in an airtight container for up to 2 days.

Add 2 tablespoons of extra lemon juice and this becomes a great companion to fish.

# MIX & MATCH

## DUMPLINGS AND DIPS CHART

I've given you my go-to pairings for each dumpling in the recipes. It's really important to match the flavors of what goes outside with what's inside. At Rickshaw, chef Anita Lo carefully composed dips to go with each dumpling. That being said, my dips are really versatile and taste great with a variety of dumplings. So you can do switcheroos whenever you want! Here are just a few more tried-and-true tasty match-ups. *HAPPY DIPPING!*

| | Soy-Vinegar Dip | Vinegar-Ginger Dip | Toasted Sesame-Soy Dip | Chile-Soy Dip |
|---|:---:|:---:|:---:|:---:|
| Watercress Beef | | ● | ● | ● |
| Butternut Squash–Corn | | | | |
| Chicken & Thai Basil | | | | |
| Chicken *Saag* | | | | |
| Chickpea | | | ● | |
| Classic Pork & Chinese Chive | ● | ● | ● | ● |
| Cumin Lamb | | | ● | |
| Pearl | | ● | ● | ● |
| Edamame | | ● | ● | ● |
| Glazed Barbecued Pork | | ● | | |
| Herby Turkey | | ● | ● | ● |
| Japanese Curry Chicken | | | | |
| Hassled Egg & Kale | | ● | ● | ● |
| Kimchi Beef | | | | |
| Lemongrass–Lime Leaf Beef | | ● | ● | ● |
| Minty Snow Pea | | ● | ● | |
| Mushroom | | ● | ● | |
| Pea Shoots & Leek | | ● | ● | ● |
| Peking Duck | | | | |
| Mom's Cilantro & Pork | ● | ● | ● | ● |
| Pork & Crab | | ● | | |
| Pork & Shrimp | | | ● | |
| Shrimp Nori | | ● | | |
| Spicy Beef & Shiso | | ● | ● | ● |
| Smashed Sweet Potato | | ● | | |
| Szechuan Chicken | | | | ● |
| Thai Green Curry | | | | |
| Mustard Greens & Mustard Seed | | ● | ● | ● |
| Szechuan Wontons in Chili Oil | | | | |
| Ma Po Tofu | | ● | ● | ● |
| Pork Shanghai Soup Dumplings | | ● | | |
| Shrimp Soup Dumplings | ● | ● | | |
| Hot & Sour Soup Dumplings | | ● | | |
| Lobster Wontons in Corn Chowder | | | | |
| Indian Street-Market | | | ● | |
| Lentil Spinach *Momos* | | | ● | ● |

| Dr.Tan's Chile Dip | Mimi Dip | Spicy Peanut Dip | Peanut Vinaigrette | Hoisin Dip | Asian Barbecue Sauce | Creamy Wasabi Dip | Lemon Sansho Dip | Lemon-Yogurt Dip | New Green Goddess Dip | Japanese Curry | Chunky Chili Oil |
|---|---|---|---|---|---|---|---|---|---|---|---|
| ● | ● |  |  | ● |  |  |  |  |  |  |  |
|  |  |  |  |  |  |  | ● | ● |  |  |  |
|  |  | ● | ● |  |  |  |  |  |  |  |  |
|  |  |  |  |  |  |  | ● | ● |  |  |  |
|  |  |  |  |  |  |  |  | ● |  |  |  |
| ● |  |  |  |  |  |  |  |  |  |  |  |
|  |  |  |  |  |  |  |  | ● |  |  |  |
| ● |  |  |  |  |  |  |  |  |  |  |  |
| ● |  |  |  |  |  |  | ● |  |  |  |  |
|  |  |  |  |  | ● |  |  |  |  |  |  |
| ● |  |  |  |  |  |  | ● |  | ● |  |  |
|  |  |  |  |  |  |  |  |  |  | ● |  |
| ● | ● |  |  | ● |  |  |  |  | ● |  |  |
|  | ● |  |  |  |  |  |  |  |  |  |  |
| ● |  | ● | ● |  |  |  |  |  |  |  |  |
|  |  |  |  |  |  |  | ● | ● |  |  |  |
| ● |  |  |  |  |  |  |  |  |  |  |  |
| ● | ● |  |  |  |  |  | ● |  | ● |  |  |
|  |  |  |  | ● |  |  |  |  |  |  |  |
| ● |  |  |  |  | ● |  |  |  |  |  |  |
|  |  |  |  |  |  |  |  |  |  |  |  |
|  |  |  |  |  |  | ● | ● | ● |  |  |  |
|  |  |  |  |  |  | ● | ● |  |  |  |  |
|  | ● |  |  |  |  |  |  | ● |  |  |  |
|  |  |  |  |  |  |  | ● |  |  |  |  |
|  |  |  |  |  |  |  |  |  |  |  |  |
| ● |  | ● | ● |  |  |  |  |  |  |  |  |
|  |  |  |  |  |  |  | ● |  |  |  |  |
|  |  |  |  |  |  |  |  |  |  |  | ● |
|  |  |  |  |  |  |  | ● |  |  |  | ● |
|  |  |  |  |  |  |  |  |  |  |  |  |
|  |  |  |  |  |  |  |  |  |  |  |  |
|  |  |  |  |  |  |  |  |  |  |  | ● |
|  |  |  |  |  |  |  |  |  |  |  | ● |
|  |  |  |  |  |  |  | ● |  |  |  |  |
|  |  |  |  |  |  |  |  | ● |  |  |  |

CHAPTER 3

BUNS & NOODLES

Chef David Chang popularized Asian-style buns in his New York City restaurants, and the trend has taken off around the world over the past decade. And for good reason. I used to live around the corner from Chang's restaurants and have stuffed my face with a fair share of Momofuku's pork buns. His versions are great, but stuffed Chinese buns aren't novel to me. I've been eating them all my life. My mom's from Taiwan, where fluffy white buns sandwiching pork belly, pickles, and peanuts are served day and night. I grew up devouring these steamy treats and have been reinventing the classic as an adult.

Sure, homemade buns are tasty, but frozen ones are actually really good too. They're easy to steam straight from the freezer and have a subtle sweetness and airy texture. Even though they're good enough to eat alone, they're way better when filled with big flavors. I like to mix it up with something salty, sour, and a touch sweet. Just about anything works, but these are my favorite combos.

The other type of bun that's less well-known here, but popular all over China, Taiwan, and Hong Kong, isn't a sandwich at all. The same type of dough is filled, then enclosed like a dumpling and steamed or pan-fried. It's like a dumpling on steroids. They're filling and fun to eat!

# STEAMED BUNS

Whenever I smell this sweet, pillowy, yeasty dough rising, I think of my grandmother. She used to make it in a dented stainless-steel bowl and feed me the buns fresh from her steamer. I've adapted her recipe to make it easy enough for all home cooks. You can use any of the fillings from the dumpling chapter; experiment to find your favorite.

1½ teaspoons active dry yeast
¾ cup (180 ml) warm water
2 tablespoons canola oil,
  plus more for the bowl

2¾ cups (385 g) all-purpose
  flour, plus more for rolling
2 tablespoons sugar
2 tablespoons baking powder

2½ cups (591 ml) dumpling
  filling of choice (pages 36
  to 97)

1  In a small bowl, sprinkle the yeast over the warm water. Let stand until the yeast is softened, about 1 minute. With chopsticks, stir in the oil.

2  In a large bowl, stir the flour (use bleached to achieve a snowy white color), sugar, and baking powder with chopsticks until well-mixed. While stirring, add the yeast mixture in a steady stream. The dough should look torn, yet plump. Transfer to a lightly floured surface and knead until smooth and elastic, about 5 minutes. When you give it your best doughboy poke, it should slowly come back and leave a small finger imprint.

3  Transfer to a lightly oiled bowl, cover loosely with plastic wrap, and let stand in a warm place until doubled in size, about 1 hour. Meanwhile, cut sixteen 3-inch (7.5-cm) squares of parchment paper.

4  Turn out the dough onto a lightly floured work surface. Cut in half and keep one half covered. Knead the other half lightly and shape into a log. Cut into eight even pieces. Cup one piece in your hand and turn it on the work surface to shape it into a 1-inch- (2.5-cm-) thick hockey puck.

5  Using a small wooden dowel, roll the puck from the center outward to form a 5-inch (12-cm)

round. Place 2 generous tablespoons filling in the center. Pick up four "corners" of the dough and pull them in toward the center so the filling can settle into the base. Pleat the wrapper between the corners to enclose the filling, then pinch the dough together right above the filling, where all the pleats meet. Pinch off any excess dough from the top. Place the bun on a piece of parchment paper and cover it with a tea towel. Repeat with the remaining dough pieces and filling. Let the filled buns sit for about 20 minutes.

6  Fill a wok with water to a depth of 3 inches (7.5 cm). You want as much water as you can get in there without it touching the bottom of the steamer, so pop the steamer on the wok and add or remove water. Bring the water to a boil.

7  Meanwhile, place the buns with their parchment paper in a bamboo steamer, spacing 2 whole inches (5 cm) apart; they expand quite a bit. Steam until the dough and filling are cooked through, 10 to 12 minutes. The dough should be shiny and bouncy when you poke it. If you're unsure whether the filling is cooked through, cut one open and take a look. Serve the buns immediately. Any leftovers can be frozen, then reheated in a steamer or microwave.

# HOW TO BUILD A BUN

These are my favorite bun recipes, but you can totally create your own too. All you have to do is buy frozen Chinese sandwich buns. (It cracks me up that they're sometimes labeled "tacos"!) Gently steam them and keep them hot in the steamer until you're ready to assemble them. The buns are fluffy, puffy, and sweet when they're hot, but turn hard and bland once they cool.

**1**

Gently steam the buns and keep them hot in the steamer until you're ready to assemble them.

**2**

Start by spreading a nice sauce on the bun (if the meat isn't already sauced). Slather it on!

**3**

Next, lay down the main filling: Peking duck; slider patty; grilled or fried beef, pork, chicken, fish, or shrimp; or roasted or sautéed hearty veggies like mushrooms, eggplant, or squash.

**4**

Top it with something fresh and green. Herbs are always a great way to go, as are slivered greens or onions or leeks.

**5**

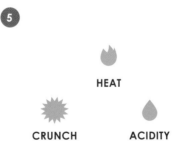

HEAT

CRUNCH    ACIDITY

To make it really special, add some crunch or heat or acidity—or all three! I'm talking roasted peanuts or fried shallots, a squirt of sriracha or drizzle of chili oil, and a squeeze of lemon or lime juice.

**6**

YUM

Imagine this: American burger meets Korean barbecue. But wait. It gets better. The patty sizzles and caramelizes with its sweet garlicky marinade, then gets stuffed into a warm bun and slathered with spicy sauce. *Yum.*

JUICY PATTY

SWEET, PILLOWY BUNS!

SPICY SAUCE

Bulgogi Bulgogi Bulgogi— It never gets boring to say.

# BULGOGI BEEF SLIDERS

MAKES 8 BUNS

1 pound (455 g) ground beef chuck
1 small onion, finely chopped
4 garlic cloves, finely chopped
3 tablespoons plus 1 teaspoon soy sauce

2 tablespoons plus 2 teaspoons sugar
2 teaspoons toasted sesame seeds
⅛ teaspoon freshly ground black pepper
8 frozen Chinese sandwich buns (see Notes, page 126), thawed

Soy or other neutral oil, as needed
Bulgogi Sauce (see below)
½ cup (65 g) matchstick-cut carrots, for serving
½ cup (52 g) bean sprouts, for serving
1 scallion, thinly sliced, for serving

1  In a large bowl, combine the beef, onion, garlic, soy sauce, sugar, sesame seeds, and pepper. Use your hands to work all the ingredients together until well-mixed. It's best to use your hands because you can get everything incorporated into the meat without making the pieces of meat too small.

2  Divide into eight even portions, then gently pat each portion into a ⅓-inch- (8-mm-) thick oval patty. The patty should be the same shape but a little bigger than a bun. When you're putting this together later, you want the patty to fit in the bun, but stick out a little around the edges. When the beef cooks, it'll shrink a little.

3  Meanwhile, prepare a steamer, preferably a bamboo one. Add the buns in a single layer, placing them 1 inch (2.5 cm) apart, and adjust the heat to maintain a bare simmer. Steam until nice and hot. You can keep the buns in the steamer until you're ready to fill them.

4  Heat a large skillet or griddle over medium-high heat. Lightly coat the pan with oil and add enough patties to fit in a single layer with space between them. Work in batches if you need to. Cook until nicely browned on both sides and cooked through in the center, about 8 minutes. Repeat with any remaining patties.

5  Take the buns out of the steamer, open them, and stuff the patties into them. Spread Bulgogi Sauce all over, and top with the carrots, bean sprouts, and scallion. Serve warm.

## BULGOGI SAUCE

MAKES ABOUT ⅓ CUP (75 ML)

¼ cup (60 ml) *gochujang* (Korean chile-bean paste)
⅓ cup (65 g) sugar

In a small bowl, whisk together the *gochujang* and sugar with 2 tablespoons water until the sugar dissolves.

# PORK BELLY BUNS WITH *CHAR SIU* SAUCE

MAKES 8 BUNS

Pork belly belongs in steamed buns. Its jiggly stripes of tender meat and juicy fat melt into the moist bread. I like to add a simple *char siu* sauce to the meat and top it with the classic Taiwanese condiments of scallions, cilantro, and peanuts.

1 pound (455 g) boneless, skin-on pork belly
Kosher salt and freshly ground black pepper
Cold water, as needed

8 frozen Chinese sandwich buns (see Notes, page 126), thawed
*Char Siu* Sauce (see below), for serving

Thinly sliced scallions, for serving
Fresh cilantro sprigs, for serving
Chopped roasted peanuts, for serving

1  Season the pork with salt and pepper and place in a medium saucepan. Add enough cold water to cover by 2 inches (5 cm). Bring to a boil over high heat, then reduce the heat to low and simmer until very tender, about 40 minutes. Using a slotted spatula, carefully transfer to a cutting board. Cut crosswise into thin slices.

2  Meanwhile, prepare a steamer, preferably a bamboo one. Add the buns in a single layer, placing them 1 inch (2.5 cm) apart, and adjust the heat to maintain a bare simmer. Steam until nice and hot. You can keep the buns in the steamer until you're ready to fill them.

3  Take the buns out of the steamer, open them, and divide the pork slices among them. Top with the sauce, scallions, cilantro, and peanuts. Serve warm.

## *CHAR SIU* SAUCE

MAKES ABOUT ⅓ CUP (75 ML)

2 tablespoons honey
2 tablespoons oyster sauce
2 tablespoons hoisin
1 tablespoon soy sauce
2 teaspoons Shaoxing wine

½ teaspoon sugar
¼ teaspoon Chinese five-spice powder
¼ teaspoon freshly ground black pepper

In a small bowl, whisk together the honey, oyster sauce, hoisin, soy sauce, wine, sugar, five-spice powder, and pepper. The sauce can be refrigerated in an airtight container for up to 3 days.

# SLOPPY ZHOU CHICKEN CURRY BUNS

MAKES 8 BUNS

At a glance, the filling looks like all-American sloppy joe. But one bite is all you need to taste the complexity that curry powder adds. Even better is the way you get to taste the flavor-packed chicken. I love when the meat gravy squishes out of the buns a little, forcing me to catch mouthfuls before they hit my shirt.

1 tablespoon vegetable oil
1 tablespoon unsalted butter
1 small onion, diced

1 pound (455 g) ground dark-meat chicken
2 tablespoons curry powder
2 tablespoons ketchup

1 tablespoon mustard
8 frozen Chinese sandwich buns (see Note, page 126), thawed

1   In a large, deep skillet, heat the oil and butter over medium-high heat until the butter melts. Add the onion and cook, stirring, until translucent and tender, about 5 minutes. Add the chicken, curry, ketchup, and mustard. Cook, stirring and breaking up the chicken into small bits, until the meat is cooked through and the mixture resembles sloppy joe meat.

2   Meanwhile, prepare a steamer, preferably a bamboo one. Add the buns in a single layer, placing them 1 inch (2.5 cm) apart, and adjust the heat to maintain a bare simmer. Steam until nice and hot. You can keep the buns in the steamer until you're ready to fill them.

3   Take the buns out of the steamer, open them, and divide the chicken filling among them. Serve warm.

Messy eating means *good times.* ☺

# SHIITAKE MUSHROOM BUNS

MAKES 8 BUNS

Fresh isn't always better. There, I said it. Sometimes, it's really true! The light earthy flavor of fresh shiitakes works beautifully in my Mushroom Dumplings (page 86), but dried shiitakes have an intensity that complements these buns better. They're almost meaty with their umami flavor, and super satisfying for vegetarians and carnivores alike.

24 dried shiitake mushrooms
Boiling water, as needed
1½ teaspoons minced peeled fresh ginger
1 tablespoon soy sauce

⅓ cup (33 g) thinly sliced scallions
8 frozen Chinese sandwich buns (see Note, page 126), thawed

Hoisin Dip (page 108), for serving
Julienned cucumber, for serving

1  Place the mushrooms in a medium heatproof bowl and cover with boiling water. Let stand until softened, about 40 minutes. Drain well, trim off and discard the stems, and squeeze out any excess liquid from the caps.

2  Meanwhile, prepare a steamer, preferably a bamboo one. Add the buns in a single layer, placing them 1 inch (2.5 cm) apart, and adjust the heat to maintain a bare simmer. Steam until nice and hot. You can keep the buns in the steamer until you're ready to fill them.

3  Prepare a second steamer or remove the buns from the first steamer. In a medium heatproof bowl, combine the mushrooms, ginger, and soy sauce. Toss until evenly coated. Sprinkle the scallions on top. Place the bowl in the steamer and steam until heated through, about 10 minutes.

4  Remove from the steamer, open the buns, and divide the mushrooms among them. Top with the hoisin dip and cucumber and serve warm.

# SWEET CHINESE SAUSAGE & EGG BUNS

MAKES 8 BUNS

During my college semester abroad in China, my best friend Bridget and I often grabbed this bun for breakfast. We'd trudge to class after a long night out and stuff our faces with this soul-warming hangover killer.

8 frozen Chinese sandwich buns, thawed (see Notes)
14 ounces (400 g) sweet Chinese sausage (see Notes), thinly sliced at an angle

8 large eggs
Kosher salt

4 scallions, thinly sliced
Sriracha or other hot sauce, for serving

1   Prepare a steamer, preferably a bamboo one. Add the buns in a single layer, placing them 1 inch (2.5 cm) apart, and adjust the heat to maintain a bare simmer. Steam until nice and hot. You can keep the buns in the steamer until you're ready to fill them.

2   Heat a medium skillet over medium-high heat. Add the sausage and cook, stirring and flipping occasionally, until the edges are crisp. Transfer to paper towels to drain. Drain all but a thin layer of fat from the pan. Reduce the heat to medium.

3   Break the eggs into the skillet and season with salt. Use a rubber spatula to break the yolks, then let them sit while the whites sizzle. As soon as the whites are almost set, stir the eggs while tilting the pan to hassle them a little. You don't want the eggs fluffy, but they should still be a little wet.

4   Take the buns out of the steamer, open them, and divide the eggs and sausage among them. Top with the scallions. Squeeze on some sriracha and serve hot.

NOTES: Asian markets stock fluffy white sandwich buns in their freezer cases. They're sometimes labeled "tacos" because of their half-moon shapes. All you need to do is steam them to heat them up, then open them and stuff!

Chinese sausage has a great firm texture and meaty sweetness. I especially like the Kam Yen Jan brand, which is available in Asian markets and even some American ones. If you can't find Chinese sausage, try this with sweet breakfast sausage links.

Because these are yeasty buns, you really do need to leave 2 whole inches (5 cm) between the buns. Steam them in batches, if needed.

# NOODLES

Slurping noodles is easily one of my favorite things to do. Doing it between bites of hot dumplings is even better! All over China, noodles and dumplings go hand-in-hand. In this carb- and gluten-phobic world, I'm bringing back the pleasure of double-carb meals.

But I'm not going totally gluttonous. My noodle dishes, including noodle soups, are really light. They're actually a refreshing counterpoint to the dumplings. You'll see that I use proportionally fewer noodles to all the other tastiness I toss in, from soups and veggies to garnishes. The noodles aren't meant to be the main part of the dish; they're there to enhance the other flavors. Once they soak up all the yummy seasonings, they're ready for you to enjoy!

# CHILLY CHILE RICE NOODLES

MAKES
8 SIDE-DISH
or
4 MAIN-DISH
SERVINGS

I was making this dish long before the gluten-free craze. Sure, that's a perk, but the real reason to make these noodles is because of the rockin' spicy, vinegary blend in the sauce. It's my go-to picnic and potluck dish, too, because it's meant to be room temp and the shredded veggies are really pretty and tasty.

Kosher salt
8 ounces (225 g) rice stick
  noodles
Canola or other neutral oil,
  as needed

½ seedless cucumber, peeled
  and julienned
1 large carrot, peeled and
  julienned
½ cup (52 g) bean sprouts
Soy-Sesame Vinaigrette (see
  below)

2 tablespoons oyster sauce
1 tablespoon sriracha
1 tablespoon black sesame
  seeds
1 scallion, thinly sliced

1 Fill a large bowl with ice and water. Bring a large saucepan of salted water to a boil. Add the noodles to the boiling water and cook until just tender, about 3 minutes. Drain and immediately transfer to the ice water. When totally cool, drain well. Make sure there aren't any hot pockets of noodles or else the delicate veg will cook when tossed in. If the noodles need to sit awhile before you're ready to serve, keep them lubed by tossing them with a little oil so they don't stick together. Oiled noodles can stand at room temperature for up to 1 hour.

2 Transfer the noodles to a large bowl and toss by loosening them with your fingers. You need to separate the strands to make it easier for the noodles to accept the other ingredients. Toss in the cucumber, carrot, and bean sprouts with your hands, then toss in the vinaigrette, oyster sauce, sriracha, and sesame seeds. Toss in the scallion just before serving.

MAKE-AHEAD TIP: If you want to prep the cucumber and carrots a day ahead of time, put them in an airtight container lined with paper towels. That'll soak up any extra moisture that would make the julienned vegetables soggy otherwise.

## SOY-SESAME VINAIGRETTE

MAKES ABOUT ⅔ CUP
  (165 ML)

2 tablespoons soy sauce
2 tablespoons rice vinegar
¾ teaspoon sugar
Pinch freshly ground black
  pepper
2 tablespoons canola oil
¼ teaspoon sesame oil

In a small bowl, whisk together the soy sauce, vinegar, sugar, and pepper. Continue whisking while adding the oils slowly until the dressing is emulsified. The dressing can be refrigerated in an airtight container for up to 1 week.

# WARM SESAME NOODLES

MAKES 8 SIDE-DISH OR 4 MAIN-DISH SERVINGS

Categorize this under Chinese-American comfort food. Countless sesame noodle recipes come straight from China, but the use of peanut butter as a noodle sauce is distinctly American. I can't get enough of this supereasy dish. You definitely don't have to wait for a party to make it. Throw it together for a yummy fast lunch or dinner!

8 ounces (225 g) fresh Shanghai-style Chinese noodles (see Note)

1 cup (260 g) creamy peanut butter

1 cup (240 ml) rice wine vinegar

⅓ cup (65 ml) soy sauce

⅓ cup (67 g) sugar

¼ cup (60 ml) very hot water

2¼ teaspoons sesame oil

Sliced scallions, for serving

Shredded cucumber, for serving

Black sesame seeds, for serving

Lime wedges, for serving

1   Cook the noodles according to the package directions. Drain well.

2   Meanwhile, in a large bowl, whisk together the peanut butter, vinegar, soy sauce, sugar, hot water, and sesame oil until smooth. Add the hot noodles and toss until well combined.

3   Top with the scallions, cucumber, and sesame seeds. Serve immediately with the lime wedges.

NOTE: Fresh Chinese noodles are available at Asian markets. You can substitute 12 ounces (340 g) thin spaghetti or linguine if you can't get them.

Kids can't stop eating this dish. And when I say kids, I mean adults.

# MISO NOODLE SOUP WITH BEAN SPROUTS

MAKES 8 SIDE-DISH SERVINGS

True miso soup starts with *dashi*, a Japanese stock, but I like it nearly as much when I make it with water. Namely because I can whip this up in less than 10 minutes that way. Skip the noodles for a lighter soup or add diced tofu for a heartier one. I love slurping this soup whenever I'm enjoying the Shrimp Nori Dumplings (page 76).

⅓ cup (90 g) white miso paste
4 ounces (115 g) Japanese soba (buckwheat) noodles
½ ounce (15 g) bean sprouts
1 tablespoon *aonori* flakes (see Note, page 76)
1 scallion, thinly sliced

1   In a large saucepan, bring 2 quarts (2 L) water to a boil. Remove from the heat.

2   In a small bowl, whisk enough of the just-boiled water into the miso paste until smooth and liquid. Return to the remaining hot water and whisk to incorporate.

3   Meanwhile, cook the noodles according to the package directions. Drain well and divide among eight serving bowls.

4   Spoon the miso soup over the noodles and top with the bean sprouts, *aonori* flakes, and scallion. Serve immediately.

Whenever I make this soup, I picture Japanese moms feeding something similar to their kids when they have the sniffles.

# CLEAR NOODLE SOUP WITH CHINESE GREENS

MAKES 8 SIDE-DISH OR 4 MAIN-DISH SERVINGS

Homemade chicken stock transforms standard take-out soup into a refined, delicious dish. The clean flavors here pair perfectly with dumplings and make this the ideal feel-better soup for stuffy noses and colds.

1 pound (455 g) chicken wings
½ ounce (15 g) fresh ginger, sliced
4 garlic cloves, peeled
2 teaspoons black peppercorns
4 scallions, chopped, plus more, thinly sliced, for serving

4 ounces (115 g) fresh Shanghai-style Chinese noodles (see Note, page 130)
¼ cup (60 ml) white soy sauce
Kosher salt and freshly ground black pepper

12 ounces (340 g) *yu choy* (see Note) or other Chinese leafy greens, trimmed
½ ounce (15 g) bean sprouts

1   In a large saucepan, cover the chicken wings with 2 quarts (2 L) water. Bring to a boil over high heat and skim off any foam that rises to the surface. Add the ginger, garlic, peppercorns, and chopped scallions. Return to a boil, then reduce the heat to maintain a steady simmer. Simmer for 3 to 4 hours.

2   Meanwhile, cook the noodles according to the package directions. Drain well and divide among serving bowls.

3   Strain the chicken stock through a sieve; discard the solids. Return to the saucepan, stir in the soy sauce, and season with salt and pepper to taste.

4   Return the stock to a boil and add the *yu choy*. Cook just until bright green and crisp-tender. Divide among the serving bowls, then spoon in the soup.

5   Top with the bean sprouts and sliced scallions and serve immediately.

NOTE: *Yu choy* is a Chinese dark green leafy vegetable that balances sweet and bitter when cooked. I especially like how tender its stems get for this soup.

Chicken wings have such a high ratio of bone to meat, they make really flavorful, rich stocks.

# THE
# ART
## OF
# EATING
# NOODLES

1. Pick up the noodles between your chopsticks with one hand and twist them on the chopsticks toward you. If you're eating dry noodles without soup, gobble them down and move on to Step 7. If your noodles are in soup, read on.

2. With your other hand, take a soupspoon and fill it partially with broth.

3. Raise the noodles high enough so the ends sit in the soupspoon.

4. Coil the noodles into the spoon and broth, still holding onto them with the chopsticks.

5. Feed the noodles into your eager mouth with the chopsticks while slurping up the soup from the spoon.

6. Wipe the splashies off your face.

7. Breathe and repeat.

# PEANUT SATÉ NOODLE SOUP WITH CRISPY SHALLOTS

MAKES 8 SIDE-DISH OR 4 MAIN-DISH SERVINGS

Do you ever wish you could drink the peanut sauce that comes with saté skewers? Yeah, me too. That's why I love this soup! It captures all those flavors in a light, creamy stock, filled with hot noodles and fresh veggies and herbs. If you want to leave all those toppings out to drink the soup alone, I won't tell.

1 pound (455 g) chicken wings
½ ounce (15 g) fresh ginger, sliced
4 garlic cloves, peeled
2 teaspoons black peppercorns
½ lemongrass stalk, smashed
4 scallions, chopped, plus more, thinly sliced, for serving
1 cup (260 g) creamy peanut butter

⅓ cup (65 ml) *nam prik pao* (roasted chile jam; see Note, page 106)
½ cup (110 g) packed brown sugar
2 tablespoons fish sauce
1½ teaspoons kosher salt
¼ teaspoon freshly ground black pepper
4 ounces (115 g) fresh Shanghai-style Chinese noodles (see Note, page 130)

Julienned cucumber, for serving
Julienned carrot, for serving
Unsweetened toasted coconut flakes, for serving
Fresh Thai basil leaves, for serving
Packaged fried shallots, for serving
Lime wedges, for serving

1   In a large saucepan, cover the chicken wings with 2 quarts (2 L) water. Bring to a boil over high heat and skim off any foam that rises to the surface. Add the ginger, garlic, peppercorns, lemongrass, and chopped scallions. Return to a boil, then reduce the heat to maintain a steady simmer. Simmer for 3 to 4 hours.

2   Strain the chicken stock through a sieve; discard the solids. Return to the saucepan and heat until steaming. Whisk in the peanut butter, *nam prik pao*, brown sugar, fish sauce, salt, and pepper until smooth. Keep warm.

3   Meanwhile, cook the noodles according to the package directions. Drain well and divide among serving bowls.

4   Spoon the soup over the noodles and top with the cucumber, carrot, coconut, basil, and shallots. Serve immediately with the lime wedges.

# PARTY MENUS

The more the merrier. That's true of both guests and food at dumpling parties. There are so many recipes in this book that rock; you could do any combo of them. But sometimes it's nice to create a menu or theme for a party. I've been doing that over the years, and this is my list of favorites. So grown-up, right? But in a totally good way.

---

### OLD-SCHOOL MENU

**Sometimes you just want the classics. For a standard but totally satisfying dumpling night, this menu delivers.**

Classic Pork & Chinese
Chive Dumplings (page 36)
Toasted Sesame–Soy Dip (page 103)
Warm Sesame Noodles (page 130)
Essential Kale Salad (page 145)
Cardamom Rice Pudding (page 195)

---

### THAI ONE ON

**Thailand's night markets thrum with an amazing good-time energy that's contagious. To capture that feeling stateside, make the dishes below. They'll bring the flavors and mouthwatering smells. All you need to do is add a rockin' soundtrack.**

Chicken & Thai Basil Dumplings
(page 63)
Spicy Peanut Dip (page 106)
Peanut Saté Noodle Soup with
Crispy Shallots (page 134)
Mango-Cilantro Salad (page 148)
Peanut Saté Salad with Coconut,
Carrot, Cucumber & Thai Basil
(page 147)
Pineapple Drinking Vinegar
(the grown-up spiked variation
for weekends!) (page 182)
Assorted ice pops
(pages 192 to 194)

## NICE DUMPLINGS AND HOT BUNS

When you really want to go all out, give 'em steaming hot dumplings and buns. Your guests will love dipping dumplings and munching on Asian-style sliders all night long.

Watercress Beef Dumplings
(page 55)
Vinegar-Ginger Dip (page 102)
Sloppy Zhou Chicken Curry Buns
(page 123)
Chilly Chile Rice Noodles (page 128)
Green Tea–Marshmallow Treats
(page 197)
Honeyed Ginger Ale (page 183)

## DAYTIME DUMPLINGS

I keep calling my parties "dumpling nights," but serving dumplings for lunch is really fun too. This collection of recipes is like edible crafting—perfect for friends who have little dumplings of their own.

*Tamago* Torta (page 151)
Herby Turkey Dumplings (page 70)
New Green Goddess Dip (page 113)
Chopstick Salad with Cucumber, Jicama & Wakame (page 142)
Minty Sun Tea (page 178)
Matcha Shortcut Shortbread
(page 196)

## SPICE NIGHT

Who likes it hot? You know you do. Gather all your chil-head buddies and hit 'em with this menu.

Szechuan Pitcher Peanuts (page 162)
Szechuan Wontons in Chili Oil
(page 38)
Spicy Tofu Salad (page 146)
Quickles (page 166)
Pork Belly Buns with *Char Siu* Sauce
(page 122)
Micheladas (page 185)

## WEEKNIGHT DUMPLINGS

This is where dumplings go from awesome weekend treat to regular weeknight repertoire. Anytime you make extra dumplings, freeze them on a sheet tray until hard, then seal them in freezer bags (see page 43). Freeze for up to 6 months and cook straight from the freezer. You're ready for an instant dumpling night any night! Who doesn't like a good dumpling on humpday?!

Mom's Cilantro & Pork Dumplings
(page 37)
Dr. Tan's Chile Dip (page 104)
Pine Nut–Corn Stir-Fry (page 150)
Essential Kale Salad (page 145)

CHAPTER 4

SALADS
&
SIDES

At my childhood dumpling parties, we always had a big salad on the side. Most of us put our hot dumplings right on the cold salad to eat together. Others kept the salads separate to munch on before, after, and during the dumpling feast. Even though we were all Chinese, we were also all Californians.

I love salads as much now as I did then. And I still tend to toss my veggies—from seaweed to leafy greens to crunchy bean sprouts—with Asian-style dressings. When I'm not in the mood for a cold salad, I go for substantial sides to eat with my dumplings. Eggs and tofu are perfectly light yet filling enough to make a dumpling feast complete.

And that's what I'm always going for—a complete feast. I have food shortage fear—as a guest and a host. Whenever I'm going to someone's place for a meal, I'm always a little worried there won't be enough for everyone. (Been there. Haven't you?) I make it a point to be a very generous host. That's why I like to put out lots of side dishes.

I go for a mix, depending on the crowd, the weather, my schedule, and my mood. I've created all of these dishes to go together in some way or another. All of the flavors work together and would taste great in whichever combination you choose.

# CHOPSTICK SALAD WITH CUCUMBER, JICAMA & WAKAME

MAKES 8 SIDE-DISH SERVINGS

The ultimate summertime salad! The crunch of the jicama and cucumber is so refreshing, and the umami in the wakame gives those lean, crisp veggies more body. At the restaurant, we used to slice the cucumber and jicama into thin rounds, but at home, I like doing sticks. My friends' kids love it that way.

2 tablespoons dried wakame (see Note)

Cold water, as needed

1 pound (455 g) seedless cucumber

1 pound (455 g) jicama

Soy-Sesame Vinaigrette (page 129)

Lime wedges, for serving

1   Put the wakame in a bowl and cover with cold water. Soak until tender, about 10 minutes, then drain well. You should have ¼ cup (60 ml).

2   Peel the cucumber in alternating strips lengthwise so it looks stripy. Cut the cucumber in half lengthwise and use a spoon to gently scoop out any seeds. Cut the halves crosswise into 4-inch- (10-cm-) long pieces, then cut each piece lengthwise into ½-inch- (12-mm-) thick sticks. Peel and cut the jicama the same size.

3   In a medium bowl, toss the cucumber, jicama, and wakame with the vinaigrette. Squeeze lime juice over just before serving.

NOTE: Wakame, a variety of seaweed, is available dried in Asian markets or online. It needs to rehydrate before use; those tiny black strips of seaweed become wide, silky ribbons after soaking in cold water. Magic!

# CITRUS-GINGER SALAD

MAKES 8 SIDE-DISH SERVINGS

At a glance, the salad dressing may look daunting because there are three different citrus juices involved. But it's so delicious, it's totally worth dealing with all three. And it's actually not such a pain. Jicama is my favorite salad addition because it adds this juicy crunch to the tender greens. Asian pear would work well here too. The secret ingredient though? Crispy Thai fried shallots. They're like the crumbles you get at the bottom of a bag of ridged potato chips. Just as salty and crunchy, but with the nice, deep sweetness of shallot. You can find them in any Asian market and eat them as a snack when you're not making this salad.

4 cups (180 g) mixed salad
  greens
1 cup (120 g) peeled and
  thinly sliced jicama
Citrus-Ginger Dressing
  (see below)
¼ cup (4 g) packaged fried
  shallots

In a salad bowl, toss the greens and jicama with just enough dressing to coat. Taste and add more dressing, if you'd like. Top with the shallots and serve immediately.

## CITRUS-GINGER DRESSING

MAKES ABOUT ½ CUP (120 ML)

¼ teaspoon freshly grated
  lime zest
¼ teaspoon freshly grated
  orange zest
1 tablespoon fresh lemon
  juice
1 tablespoon fresh lime juice
1 tablespoon fresh orange
  juice
1 teaspoon minced onion

1 teaspoon sugar
¾ teaspoon soy sauce
¾ teaspoon kosher salt
¼ teaspoon grated peeled
  fresh ginger
⅛ teaspoon finely chopped
  garlic
Pinch freshly ground black
  pepper
⅓ cup (65 ml) soybean oil

In a small bowl, whisk together the citrus zests and juices, onion, sugar, soy sauce, salt, ginger, garlic, and pepper. Continue whisking while adding the oil slowly until the dressing is emulsified. Taste it and adjust the seasonings to your taste. You can refrigerate the dressing in an airtight container for up to 5 days.

# ESSENTIAL KALE SALAD

MAKES 8 SIDE-DISH SERVINGS

Kale, kale, kale. I feel like there must be some kale marketing board paying everyone to gush about this wonder veg. I will not gush, but I will say that I love how well kale holds up when dressed. I can massage dressing into the leaves in the morning and the salad still tastes great at night. That makes it a great accompaniment when entertaining or even on a weekday evening. All hail the kale!

¼ cup (60 ml) Ginger-Soy Dressing (see below) or Peanut Vinaigrette (page 107), plus more to taste
6 cups (120 g) torn kale leaves without stems, washed and dried well
1 ripe avocado, diced
1 lemon, cut into wedges
¼ cup (25 g) toasted chopped almonds
Peeled and thinly sliced carrots, for garnish

1  In a large bowl, massage the dressing into the kale with your fingers until very well mixed and the leaves are tenderized, about 2 minutes. The dressed leaves can be covered and refrigerated for up to 6 hours.

2  Right before serving, massage the avocado into the leaves, then squeeze in some lemon juice. Taste and add more dressing if needed. Top with the almonds and carrots and serve.

## GINGER-SOY DRESSING

MAKES ABOUT ½ CUP (120 ML)

¼ cup (60 ml) soy sauce
1½ tablespoons rice wine vinegar
1½ tablespoons sesame seeds
½ teaspoon sugar
½ teaspoon minced garlic
1 teaspoon minced peeled fresh ginger

In a small bowl, whisk together the soy sauce, vinegar, sesame seeds, sugar, garlic, ginger, and 2 tablespoons water. The dressing can be stored in an airtight container for up to 3 days.

If you make this for a weekday dinner and have leftovers, you now have kale salad for tomorrow's lunch, and it just gets better! Who ever heard of a lettuce-type salad getting better the next day? Whoa!

# SPICY TOFU SALAD

I think of this as a hot salad, but you could definitely serve it as a side or even as a main dish for vegetarians. The chili oil brings a big jolt of flavor to the subtlety (okay, blandness) of plain tofu, while bean sprouts add crunch.

1 pound (455 g) firm tofu, drained and cut into 1-inch (2.5-cm) slices (like steak)

3 tablespoons canola oil

2 cups (210 g) bean sprouts

½ cup (50 g) julienned scallions

3 tablespoons Chunky Chili Oil (page 38), or to taste

1   Place the tofu slices between sheets of paper towels. Put a pan on top and weigh it down to drain all of the excess liquid. Cut the slices into 1-inch (2.5-cm) cubes.

2   In a large nonstick skillet, heat the oil over medium-high heat until hot but not smoking. Add the tofu in a single layer. Fry, turning to evenly brown on all sides, 10 to 15 minutes. Drain on paper towels.

3   In a large bowl, toss the tofu, bean sprouts, and scallions with the chili oil. Serve immediately.

Drain as much liquid as you can out of the tofu, replacing the paper towels as needed. The drier the tofu, the crisper it becomes when fried!

When you know vegetarians are coming to dinner, be sure to have this side dish on the table!

# PEANUT SATÉ SALAD WITH COCONUT, CARROT, CUCUMBER & THAI BASIL

MAKES 8 SIDE-DISH SERVINGS

I'm always looking for an excuse to eat my Spicy Peanut Dip (page 106). Fresh veggies are pretty much the best reason I'll ever have. Well, that and the Chicken & Thai Basil Dumplings (page 63). When I don't have a stash of those in the freezer, I toss together this easy salad to get my fix.

1 cup (240 ml) Spicy Peanut Dip (page 106)

1 tablespoon fresh lemon juice

2 cups (240 g) julienned cucumber

1 cup (130 g) julienned carrot

½ cup (50 g) julienned scallions

¼ cup (20 g) unsweetened coconut flakes, toasted

Fresh Thai basil leaves, for serving

Lime wedges, for serving

In a large bowl, whisk the peanut dip and lemon juice until smooth. Add the cucumber, carrot, scallions, and coconut. Toss until well-mixed. Top with the basil leaves and serve immediately with lime wedges.

This goes great with Chicken & Thai Basil Dumplings (page 63).

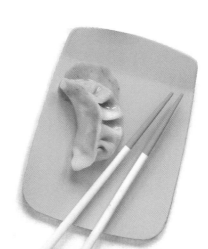

# HERBY SALAD

━━━━━━━━━━━━━━━━━

MAKES 8 SIDE-DISH SERVINGS

In China, restaurants often plop a cilantro condiment on the table along with steaming dumplings. This is my salad-ization of that little side dish. It's kind of a cross between a salad and a pickle, actually. I love pecking at these awesomely aromatic greens with my chopsticks between bites of spicy-hot fried dumplings.

2 cups (50 g) chopped fresh cilantro

4 scallions, cut into 2-inch (5-cm) batons

4 celery stalks, thinly sliced at an angle

2 tablespoons rice wine vinegar

1 tablespoon fresh lime juice

1½ teaspoons soy sauce

½ teaspoon kosher salt

¼ teaspoon sugar

¼ teaspoon freshly ground black pepper

In a large bowl, toss together all of the ingredients until very well mixed. Serve immediately or refrigerate in an airtight container for up to 1 day.

# MANGO-CILANTRO SALAD

━━━━━━━━━━━━━━━━━

MAKES 8 SIDE-DISH SERVINGS

This sweet chunky salad is great on its own. If you want to turn it into a main meal, it's fantastic on top of greens. My favorite way of serving it though, is as a side to spicy hot dishes.

2 tablespoons fresh lime juice

1 tablespoon fish sauce

1 tablespoon honey

1 fresh red Thai chile (see Note), stemmed, seeded, and minced

4 ripe but firm mangoes, peeled, pitted, and cut into 1-inch (2.5-cm) chunks

2 tablespoons finely chopped scallions

2 tablespoons finely chopped fresh cilantro, plus sprigs for garnish

In a large nonreactive bowl, whisk the lime juice, fish sauce, honey, and chile. Toss in the mangoes, scallions, and cilantro. Let stand for 30 minutes. Toss again and serve.

NOTE: If you don't have fresh Thai red chiles, use a pinch of crushed red chile flakes instead.

# WATERMELON & MINT SALAD

MAKES 8 SIDE-DISH SERVINGS

Watermelon is one of my top-ten desert island foods. As a kid, I was amazed at how crunchy watermelon would burst into juiciness the second I bit into it. As a grown-up, I'm amazed at how the texture maintains that crunchy-juicy balance even after being marinated. In fact, I like making this ahead of time because the lime juice, rum, and salt do wonders to the watermelon.

9 cups (1.4 kg) 2-inch (5-cm) watermelon cubes
¼ cup (60 ml) fresh lime juice
2 tablespoons dark rum (optional)
¼ teaspoon kosher salt
Pinch cayenne pepper
½ cup (12 g) fresh mint leaves

1  In a large bowl, gently toss the watermelon, lime juice, rum (if using), salt, and cayenne until evenly coated. Cover and let stand for at least 15 minutes and up to 6 hours.

2  Right before serving, thinly slice the mint leaves and toss them into the salad until evenly distributed.

# PINE NUT–CORN STIR-FRY

MAKES 8 SIDE-DISH SERVINGS

The crunch of end-of-summer corn combined with savory pops of rich pine nuts blows me away. When you throw the two together in a hot pan, you get an alpine sort of aroma going on. When the corn rocks its sweetness, I rock it right back with this stir-fry.

2 tablespoons grapeseed oil
1 fresh Thai red chile, stemmed, seeded, and minced (see Note, page 148)
¼ cup (30 g) finely diced red onion

4 cups (580 g) fresh corn kernels
1 teaspoon kosher salt
1 cup (135 g) pine nuts, toasted

2 tablespoons mushroom soy sauce or liquid aminos
2 tablespoons fresh lime juice
¼ cup (25 g) thinly sliced scallions, for serving

1   Heat a large skillet or wok over medium-high heat until hot. Add the oil and heat. Add the chile and half the onion. Let sit for 1 minute. Add the corn and give it a good stir. Add the salt and cook, stirring, for 2 minutes.

2   Toss in the pine nuts, soy sauce or liquid aminos, and lime juice, then transfer to a serving dish. Top with the scallions and remaining onion. Serve immediately.

# *TAMAGO* **TORTA**

MAKES 8 SIDE-DISH SERVINGS

Mash-up time! Japanese sweet omelet meets savory Spanish tortilla. Herb-scented eggs bind together fried sweet potatoes and onion in this simple skillet side. In traditional Spanish tortillas, both sides are cooked with a tricky egg-flipping technique. I've skipped that step by simply covering the eggs while they cook. You can have this as a main meal for breakfast, lunch, or dinner and, of course, as a side dish at a dumpling party. This is great for picnics too, because it travels well and is meant to be served cold or at room temperature.

12 large eggs
3 tablespoons mirin
2 tablespoons sugar
1 teaspoon kosher salt

1 teaspoon fresh thyme leaves
1 cup (240 ml) canola oil
½ small onion, very thinly sliced

1 pound (455 g) sweet potatoes, peeled and cut into 1-inch (2.5-cm) chunks

1 In a large bowl, whisk the eggs, mirin, sugar, salt, and thyme. Set aside.

2 Heat the oil in a nonstick 10-inch (25-cm) skillet over medium heat until hot but not smoking. Add the onion and sweet potatoes. Cook, turning occasionally, until the sweet potatoes are soft and light brown, 10 to 12 minutes. Strain through a sieve, reserving the potato mixture and oil separately.

3 Return 1 tablespoon oil to the skillet and heat over medium heat. Add the egg mixture, then the sweet potato mixture. Fold together until well mixed, then spread out evenly. Cover and cook without hassling it until the eggs are cooked through. The torta will brown and possibly even blacken on the pan side, but it'll taste fine.

4 Remove from the heat and center a large serving plate on top of the skillet. Quickly and carefully flip both the skillet and plate together, then lift off the skillet.

5 Let the torta cool to room temperature. Serve at room temperature or cover with plastic wrap and refrigerate up to overnight to serve cold. Cut into slices before serving.

Remember: Room temp dishes rule for parties! That makes this the perfect hearty side for vegetarians—and meat eaters too.

# CHILLED TOFU WITH SCALLION & SOY-SESAME VINAIGRETTE

MAKES 8 SIDE-DISH SERVINGS

All over East Asia, this dead-simple dish finds its way onto family tables. The best versions start with from-scratch tofu, but high-quality store-bought tofu works well too. The vinaigrette seasons each bite of this refreshing side dish.

1 pound (455 g) silken tofu, cut into 1-inch (2.5-cm) slices

¼ cup (60 ml) Soy-Sesame Vinaigrette (see page 129)

¼ cup (25 g) thinly sliced scallions

2 tablespoons black sesame seeds

1 Arrange the tofu slices on a serving dish and refrigerate until chilled.

2 Pour the vinaigrette over the tofu and top with the scallions and sesame seeds. Serve cold.

# DUMPLINGS
## BY
# NAME

When you order dumplings in most Asian restaurants, eight times out of ten you will see the word "dumpling" on the menu. But what if you see *shui jiao* or *guotie*? This guide will help you parse all of it out and understand that a dumpling by any other name is still delicious.

### JIAOZI

Literally means "horn." Makes sense since they're shaped like rams' horns. This is the most general term for dumplings of all types.

### SHUI JIAO

Literally means "water dumplings" because these are boiled.

### ZHENGJIAO

Literally means "steamed dumplings" because, well...do I even have to say it?

### GUOTIE

Literally means "pan metal," or as we'd say in English, "potsticker." These dumplings are pan-fried to a beautiful crisp on one side.

### PEKING RAVIOLI

Chef Joyce Chen's attempt in the 1950s to make dumplings relatable to her Italian neighborhood customers in Boston.

### WONTON

Literally means "swallowing clouds." Just a bit of filling goes into very thin square wrappers so lots of pillowy, soft pasta surrounds these delicate dumplings. They can be served swimming in soup or alone when deep-fried.

### GYOZA

Japanese for "dumpling." These are usually pan-fried, but sometimes come steamed.

### NORTHERN-STYLE

Northern- or Beijing-style dumplings traditionally have thicker wheat-flour skins and hearty old-school fillings, such as pork with garlicky Chinese chives.

### SOUTHERN-STYLE

Southern-style dumplings in China have fewer ingredients and focus more on the meat itself. They also typically have thinner skins, sometimes made from egg-based doughs.

# CHAPTER 5

FINGER
FOODS
&
SNACKS

I grew up obsessed with snack time. As a kid, I used to fantasize about having a clock that would ring for snack time. And it'd be ringing pretty much nonstop. As a grown-up, I still obsess over snacks. Honestly, it's too embarrassing for me to tell you my guilty-pleasure supermarket munchies. But I can tell you that all the homemade bites here are tastier than anything store-bought. I can't imagine throwing a party without little dishes to start.

I always kick off a dumpling party by setting out these snacks along with drinks. Even if you're not throwing a party, you'll want to make these yummers to eat anytime. I've made them irresistible by toeing the line between salty and sweet and adding a touch of heat here and there. Some recipes are more involved than others, but they can all be made ahead, served at room temperature, and eaten with fingers. If that doesn't make entertaining easy, I don't know what does.

# HERBY SUMMER ROLLS

MAKES 16 ROLLS

Think of these as a super fresh pre-dumpling dumpling. Colorful crunchy veggies and herbs and chewy noodles shine through rice paper wrappers. They're perfect for steamy summer days!

**FOR THE PEANUT SAUCE:**
½ cup (130 g) creamy peanut
  butter
½ cup (120 ml) rice wine
  vinegar
2½ tablespoons soy sauce
2½ tablespoons sugar

**FOR THE SUMMER ROLLS:**
Kosher salt
1 (1-pound/455-g) package
  rice stick noodles

¼ cup (60 ml) fresh lime juice
1 tablespoon rice wine
  vinegar
1 teaspoon sugar
2 cups (220 g) shredded
  carrots
2 cups (240 g) shredded
  cucumbers
Hot water, as needed
16 (8-inch/20-cm) round rice
  paper wrappers

½ small jicama, peeled and
  cut into ½-inch (12-mm)
  sticks
¼ cup (25 g) thinly sliced
  scallions
¼ cup (6 g) fresh cilantro
  sprigs
¼ cup (6 g) fresh mint leaves
¼ cup (6 g) fresh basil
  leaves

1 **Make the peanut sauce:** In a small bowl, whisk together the peanut butter, vinegar, soy sauce, and sugar until smooth and the sugar dissolves. Transfer to a serving bowl.

2 **Make the rolls:** Fill a large bowl with ice and water. Bring a large saucepan of salted water to a boil. Add the noodles to the boiling water and cook until just tender, about 3 minutes. Drain and immediately transfer to the ice water. When totally cool, drain well.

3 In a medium bowl, whisk the lime juice, vinegar, and sugar until the sugar dissolves. Add the carrots and cucumbers and toss to evenly coat.

4 Fill a large bowl with hot water. Place one rice paper wrapper in the hot water and let sit until just softened and pliable. Transfer to a cutting board. Place a line of noodles in the center and top with one jicama stick, some carrots and cucumbers, scallions, cilantro, mint, and basil. Fold in the ends of the wrapper, then roll up tightly like a burrito. Transfer to a serving dish. Repeat with the remaining wrappers and filling, spacing the finished rolls ½ inch (12 mm) apart.

5 Serve the rolls with the peanut sauce for dipping or store in the fridge for up to 1 day.

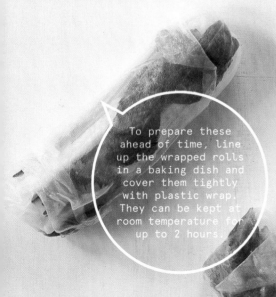

To prepare these ahead of time, line up the wrapped rolls in a baking dish and cover them tightly with plastic wrap. They can be kept at room temperature for up to 2 hours.

# UMAMI POPCORN

MAKES 8 TO 12 SNACK SERVINGS

There is something so comforting about eating popcorn. Whether it reminds you of the circus, a Saturday matinee, or a rainy movie night at home, popcorn is one of those snacks that brings people together. And it's even better when there's the added savory crunch of toasted sesame seeds and seaweed. The classic Japanese topper, known as *nori furikake*, also tastes great simply sprinkled over steamed rice. I even use it in my Hassled Eggs & Kale Dumplings (page 85). It has that mouthwatering umami that makes it totally irresistible. (Not that popcorn needs to get any more addictive!)

**FOR THE *NORI FURIKAKE*:**
4 sheets nori (roasted seaweed)
¼ cup (35 g) black sesame seeds
¼ cup (35 g) white sesame seeds

1 teaspoon kosher salt
¼ cup (3 g) bonito flakes, chopped
¼ teaspoon sugar
Freshly ground black pepper

**FOR THE POPCORN:**
¼ cup (60 ml) canola oil
½ cup (100 g) popcorn kernels
3 tablespoons unsalted butter

1   **Make the *nori furikake*:** Cut the nori into 2½-inch (6-cm) strips, then cut each strip into ¼-inch (6-mm) slices. Set aside.

2   In a small skillet, heat the black and white sesame seeds over medium-high heat. Cook, stirring and tossing occasionally, until fragrant and crackling. Don't let them burn! Immediately transfer the seeds to a large bowl and toss with the salt. Let cool completely.

3   Add the bonito flakes, sugar, and nori. Toss until well-mixed and season with pepper to taste. The *nori furikake* can be stored in an airtight container at room temperature for up to 5 days.

4   **Make the popcorn:** In a large Dutch oven with a lid, combine the oil and 3 popcorn kernels. Set the pot over medium-high heat. When the kernels pop, add the remaining kernels, cover, and remove the pot from the heat. Count to 30.

5   Turn the heat back on to medium-high, adjust the lid so it's slightly ajar, and cook the kernels, vigorously shaking the pan occasionally. Keep cooking and shaking until the popping slows to 2 to 3 seconds apart. Pour the popcorn into a large bowl. Add the butter to the pot and let it melt, then pour it over the popcorn. Toss until the popcorn is evenly coated.

6   Sprinkle on just enough *nori furikake* to speckle the popcorn; reserve the remainder for your next batch. Serve fresh.

To keep guests from fighting over who gets to hold the bowl, serve the popcorn in a bunch of little bowls.

# THE
# YUMMIEST HISTORY
## YOU'LL EVER READ

**206 BCE–220 CE**

### THEY LIKE IT!
An imperial chef of the Han dynasty (206 BCE–220 CE) inadvertently created *guotie* (pan-fried dumplings; see Dumplings by Name on page 153) when he burned one side of a batch. Then he went ahead and served them that way. Those lucky inner court members were the first to taste the crackly goodness of fried dumplings.

**150–219 CE**

### SAY AHHHH
Famed Han dynasty medicinal sage (a.k.a. superwise doctor) Zhang Zhongjing (150–219 CE) created an edible starchy packet filled with herbs and lamb that was served in a hot broth to cure sickness.

**1254–1324 CE**

### MARCO POLO
Rumor has it that Marco Polo (1254–1324 CE) was responsible for bringing Chinese noodles and dumplings to his home country of Italy and filling them with cheese and covering them with tomatoes. In reality, there is evidence that pasta made from flour existed in Europe before Marco Polo's journey, brought there by other merchants who traveled the Silk Road.

**1815**

### BOOK 'EM
On June 26, 1815, Eliza Fenning, a household servant from London, was wrongfully sent to the gallows when accused of poisoning her employers by putting white arsenic in their dumplings. This was a seminal case for the use of forensic evidence.

**2014**

### JUST CAN'T GET ENOUGH
In 2014, Joey Chestnut set a new world record by eating 384 chicken and vegetable dumplings (without soy sauce) in ten minutes. That's a lot of dumplings.

# EDAMAME WITH SANSHO PEPPER SALT

MAKES 8 TO 12 SNACK SERVINGS

Edamame make the best party starter! They couldn't be easier, and the bright bite of Japanese sansho pepper adds a nice kick to the little beans. You can skip it if you can't find it. The salt is key. Once your guests start licking their fingers, they'll be ready to party.

¼ teaspoon kosher salt, plus
  more as needed
8 ounces (225 g) frozen
  edamame in pods, thawed
Pinch Japanese sansho pepper

1 Bring a large pot of salted water to a boil. Add the edamame and cook until just heated through, 1 to 2 minutes. Drain well and transfer to a serving bowl.

2 Combine the salt and sansho pepper and sprinkle over the edamame.

# SZECHUAN PITCHER PEANUTS

MAKES ABOUT 4 CUPS (580 G)

I call these "pitcher peanuts" because you're gonna need to guzzle a pitcher of something while you munch. (May as well be chilly-willy beer.) It's the Szechuan peppercorns that will make your mouth water. They've only recently been allowed in the U.S. legally. Just a decade ago, you could get them only from chile-loving chefs who snuck them into the country. Their magic lies in their lip-numbing effect and distinct floral peppery flavor. These super spicy nuts will get your tongue tingling for dumplings!

2 tablespoons Szechuan
  peppercorns
1 teaspoon coriander seeds
1 teaspoon fennel seeds

1 orange
2 tablespoons canola oil
1 teaspoon cayenne pepper
1 dried red chile, seeded and
  very thinly sliced

4 cups (580 g) unsalted
  peanuts
Kosher salt

1   In a large skillet, heat the peppercorns, coriander seeds, and fennel seeds over medium heat until fragrant and toasted. Transfer to a spice grinder and let cool completely, then grind into a fine powder.

2   While the spices cool, remove one-quarter of the orange zest in strips with a vegetable peeler, then very thinly slice to match the thickness of the chile slices.

3   Line a large rimmed baking sheet with paper towels and place next to the stove. In the same skillet you used to toast the spices, heat the oil over medium-high heat. Add the ground spices, orange zest, cayenne pepper, and chile. Cook, stirring, just until aromatic. Don't let anything burn! Add the peanuts and cook, stirring, until well-coated and toasted, 2 to 3 minutes. Season with salt and toss well.

4   Transfer to the lined tray and let cool completely. The peanuts can be stored in an airtight container at room temperature for up to 5 days.

Eat these with a pitcher of icy Michelada (page 185).

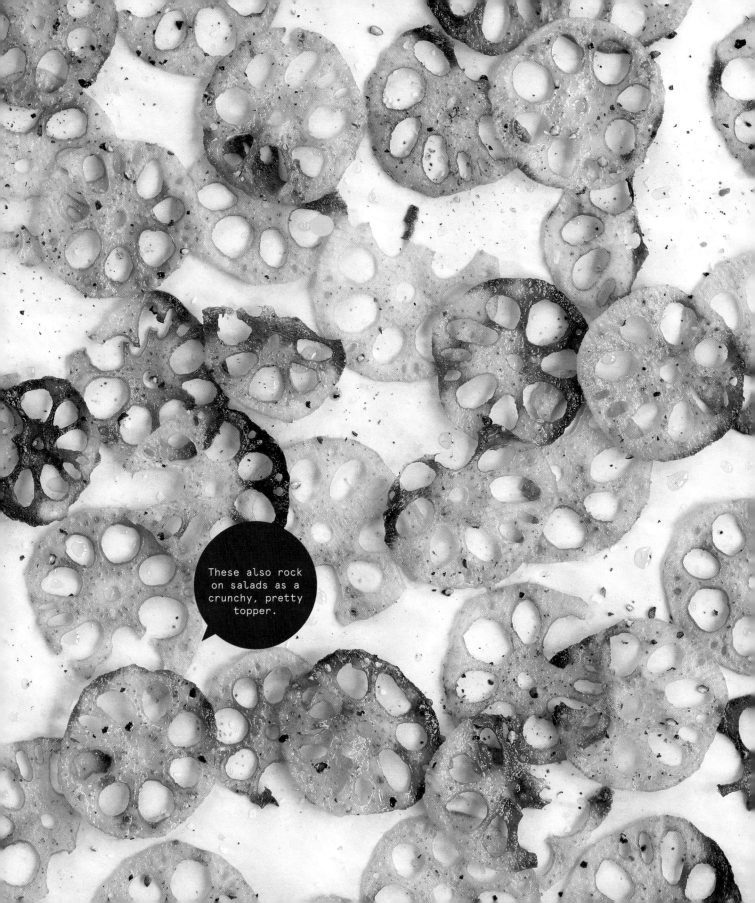

# LOTUS ROOT CHIPS

MAKES 8 TO 12 SNACK SERVINGS

**What's fantastic about these "chips" is that they bake in the oven. No messy deep-frying! Woohoo! The other thing about them is how pretty they look. Lotus roots are starchy vegetables run through with little tunnels. When you slice them paper-thin (with a mandoline, if you have one), you see these beautiful patterns. Just try not to down them all before you get them to the table!**

1 lotus root (12 ounces/340 g), peeled and sliced crosswise as thinly as possible
Cold water, as needed
2 tablespoons extra-virgin olive oil
1 teaspoon sesame oil
¾ teaspoon kosher salt
½ teaspoon freshly ground black pepper
⅛ teaspoon chili powder (optional)

1   Preheat the oven to 375°F (190°C). Line two rimmed baking sheets with parchment paper.

2   In a large bowl, cover the lotus root slices with cold water. Let stand for 30 minutes. Drain well and pat dry between paper towels. Dry the bowl and return the lotus root slices. Add the olive and sesame oils and toss until the lotus is evenly coated. Toss in the salt, pepper, and chili powder, if using.

3   Divide the slices between the prepared baking sheets and arrange in single layers.

4   Bake until golden brown and crispy, 15 to 18 minutes. When you check them, they may be a bit soft in the center, but they will crisp up as they cool down. Transfer the lotus root slices to a wire rack to cool completely. The chips can be stored in an airtight container at room Temperature for up to 1 week.

# QUICKLES

MAKES 8 SIDE-DISH SERVINGS

The crunchiness and spiky high notes of these fast pickles make this a side dish I turn out on a weekly basis. The coolness and acidity go great with hot crunchy foods like pan-fried dumplings. Once I make the recipe, it is so easy to just add vegetables to the leftover liquid. Double duty!

1 cup (115 to 145 g) very thinly sliced vegetables, such as French breakfast radishes, Daikon radish, peppers, celery, or beets

½ cup (67 g) kosher salt
3 tablespoons rice wine vinegar or fresh lemon juice

2 garlic cloves, smashed
1 teaspoon Szechuan peppercorns, toasted and crushed
1 teaspoon honey

1  In a small bowl, toss the vegetables with the salt. Transfer to a small colander, set over the bowl, and let stand for 1 hour.

2  Rinse the vegetables under cold water and drain very well by patting dry with paper towels or spinning in a salad spinner.

3  Transfer the vegetables to a medium nonreactive bowl and toss in the vinegar or lemon juice, garlic, peppercorns, and honey. Cover and refrigerate for at least 30 minutes and up to 3 days. Serve cool.

Use a mandoline if you have one to quickly cut the veggies into perfect, even, superthin slices.

Garlic lovers always fight over the pickley cloves!

FRENCH
BREAKFAST
RADISHES

PEPPERS

DAIKON
RADISHES

CARROTS

CELERY

BEETS

# OUTDOOR RICE DUMPLINGS

MAKES 9 DUMPLINGS

*Onigiri* is the real name of these Japanese rice packets, but I like to call them outdoor rice dumplings because I always ate them outside the house. These were one of the awesome car treats my mom made when we went on road trips. They travel really well because moist sushi rice stays soft at room temperature and holds pretty much any filling inside. To keep your hands from getting sticky when you're nibbling on these, you can even wrap a strip of savory toasted seaweed around the rice!

1 cup (205 g) uncooked sushi rice, washed until the water runs clear

2 tablespoons rice wine vinegar

1 teaspoon sugar

½ teaspoon kosher salt

1 teaspoon canola oil

1 (8-ounce/225-g) skin-on salmon fillet

2 tablespoons mirin

2 toasted nori sheets, cut into nine 3-inch-(7.5-cm-) wide strips

1   In a large saucepan, cover the rice with 1½ cups (360 ml) water. Bring to a boil, stir well, then cover. Reduce the heat to maintain a low simmer and simmer, covered, until the rice is tender, about 15 minutes.

2   While the rice cooks, arrange an oven rack 6 inches (15 cm) from the broiler heat source and preheat the broiler.

3   Fluff the rice with a fork or chopsticks. Gently fold in the vinegar, sugar, and salt with a rice paddle or large spatula. Do not overmix and break the rice. Let cool slightly.

4   While the rice cools, heat the oil in an ovenproof skillet over medium-high heat. Add the salmon, skin-side down, and cook for 3 minutes. Turn the salmon over and add the mirin. Be careful! The liquid will sizzle and spit. Use the skillet lid as a shield if you need to. Cook the salmon for another 3 minutes, then transfer the skillet to the broiler.

5   Broil just until the salmon skin is crisp, 1 to 2 minutes. Transfer the salmon to a cutting board and cut into small pieces with the crisp skin.

6   With damp hands, gently form ⅓ cup (75 ml) of the rice into a ball and make an indentation in the center. Fill with a piece of salmon and enclose with the surrounding rice. Dampen your hands again and shape the filled rice into a 1-inch-(2.5-cm-) thick triangle. Wrap a strip of nori around the triangle. Repeat with the remaining rice, filling, and nori. Serve at room temperature.

# THAI BEEF JERKY

MAKES ABOUT 8 OUNCES (225 G)
ENOUGH FOR A COUPLE TO SURVIVE A 6-HOUR ROAD TRIP!

As a kid, I often visited my extended family in Thailand. The best part of coming out of the water on Thailand's Pattaya beaches was knowing I could buy—and devour—freshly made beef jerky. It was chewy in the center, crispy and salty on the outside. And the savory meat was permeated with just a hint of sweetness. It's a meat-lover's dream snack!

1 teaspoon coriander seeds
½ teaspoon black peppercorns
2 tablespoons finely chopped fresh lemongrass
2 tablespoons finely chopped fresh cilantro stems

1 tablespoon finely chopped garlic
1 teaspoon sugar
½ teaspoon kosher salt, plus more as needed
2 tablespoons fish sauce

1 pound (455 g) flank steak, thinly sliced against the grain
1 cup (240 ml) canola oil

1  Preheat the oven to 180°F (80°C). Fit a wire rack into a rimmed baking sheet.

2  In a spice grinder, pulse the coriander seeds and peppercorns until finely ground. Add the lemongrass, cilantro, garlic, sugar, and salt. Pulse until finely ground. Transfer to a large bowl and stir in the fish sauce. Add the steak and massage the marinade into the meat.

3  Arrange the meat strips in a single layer on the rack in the pan. Place the pan in the oven, leaving the oven door ajar. Bake for 4 hours. The meat should be cooked through and still be moist.

4  In a large, heavy, deep skillet, heat the oil over medium-high heat until hot but not smoking. Add just enough meat to fit comfortably in a single layer and cook until darkened and fragrant, 2 to 3 minutes per side. Drain on paper towels and immediately sprinkle with salt to taste.

5  Serve hot, warm, or at room temperature. The beef jerky can be refrigerated in an airtight container for up to 2 weeks.

Of course, I serve this as a cocktail snack with drinks, but it's also great as a condiment on top of rice. Quick weeknight meal!

These are great for
bringing to a party, potluck,
or picnic!

# CHINESE TEA EGGS

MAKES 8 EGGS

Hard-boiled eggs rise to a whole other level of deliciousness when steeped in aromatic tea. The shell-cracking step may seem fussy, but it ensures that the eggs soak up the tea mixture while creating a pretty pattern on the eggs.

8 large eggs
Cold water, as needed
¼ cup (60 ml) soy sauce
3 bags black Chinese tea
½ cinnamon stick
3 dried orange peels (see Note)
1 teaspoon kosher salt

1 In a large saucepan, cover the eggs by 1 inch (2.5 cm) with cold water. Bring to a boil, reduce the heat, and simmer for 3 minutes. Drain well, rinse under cold water until cool, and drain again.

2 With a metal spoon, gently tap the eggs all over to create webs of cracks without actually cracking and removing the egg shells.

3 In the same saucepan, combine the soy sauce, tea bags, cinnamon, orange peels, salt, and 2 cups (480 ml) water. Bring to a boil, then gently place the eggs in the mixture. Bring to a boil again, then reduce the heat to low and simmer the eggs gently for 1 hour. Remove from the heat. Cover and let steep for 2 more hours.

4 Serve warm or at room temperature. Leftover eggs can be refrigerated in an airtight container for up to 3 days.

NOTE: Dried orange peels are available at Chinese markets. You can use strips of fresh orange zest if you can't find the dried peel.

# PARTY-PLANNING TIPS

Don't make dumplings alone. They're way more fun to wrap with people you love! Second only to the pleasure of eating them is the joy of making dumplings with friends. It gives your hands something to do while you hang out. And, of course, a delicious meal to share at the end. Even though your guests will be getting messy with you in the kitchen, you don't want to show them everything behind the curtain. Here's a quick checklist to prep for your party:

### 1 TO 2 NIGHTS AHEAD

Make the dumpling filling, press plastic wrap directly on the surface, cover tightly, and refrigerate. This way, the flavors get a chance to hang out and meld together, and the filling's easier to wrap when it's nice and cold.

If you keep your stash of dumpling wrappers in the freezer, defrost them overnight in the fridge.

Stir the dipping sauces and seal them in airtight containers in the fridge.

Get everything ready for your drinks. Buy the booze, macerate fruit, squeeze citrus juices, simmer and chill simple syrups, and steep vinegars. Mix up anything except the bubblies and keep everything cold in the fridge.

### 4 TO 8 HOURS AHEAD

Make any side dishes, snacks, soups, or desserts that can hold for a while.

### 3 HOURS AHEAD

Make yourself a drink. You can't take care of guests unless you take care of yourself. Besides (if you really need an excuse to get started), you should road-test your cocktails and drinks before serving them.

Get yourself a snack. I'm definitely not recommending you drink on an empty stomach. You don't want to be drunk—or "hangry"—when your guests arrive. Remember, it's going to be at least 45 minutes before that first batch of dumplings is ready. On the other hand, hunger motivates people to wrap dumplings super fast!

Turn on some tunes. Nothing like a little heartfelt soul from my man Bill Withers to get you pumped and passionate about your dumplings!

## 2 HOURS AHEAD

Clear and clean a flat work surface. Choose a surface that's easy to wipe down. You want to keep sanitizing it as you're all wrapping to avoid any cross-contamination or other icky germs. If you have a countertop, arrange stools on both sides so guests can sit while wrapping.

Divide your dipping sauces among small serving bowls. Keep any extra nearby so you're ready to refill. It's okay to leave them at room temperature at this point. Actually, it's better. You can taste the nuanced flavors more readily that way.

Set up your dumpling wrapping station as described on pages 22 to 23. To make your guests comfortable, be sure to have everything within arm's reach. For every two to four guests, plan on one bowl of filling and one package of wrappers in the center and one parchment paper–lined pan for finished dumplings. Keep the filling and wrappers in the fridge until everyone arrives, but have them all good to go. Each person should get his or her own spoon or knife for the filling, a finger bowl filled with water for wetting the wrappers, and a kitchen towel for wiping hands and the surface. If you're going the homemade Wheat Flour Wrappers (page 47) route, each person should also have a dowel and small bowl of flour.

Then set up a cooking station with pans for frying or steamers for steaming.

## 1 HOUR AHEAD

Set out serving ware, including chopsticks, small plates and bowls, and napkins. Keep forks and spoons handy for those who can't handle chopsticks. I like to keep it casual and just pile them buffet-style.

Put the finishing touches on snacks, side dishes, and soups, then arrange them in serving dishes.

Wrap a few dumplings as models for guests to see what their finished products should look like. Keep them in the fridge if everyone is running late.

## DING-DONG

Smile for that random guest who gets there on
the dot.

Scrub-a-dub: Have your guests wash their
hands well.

Get 'em all a drink.

Crack open this awesome book to pages 24 to
29 so they can see what they're supposed to do.
Don't worry if it gets all splattered and gunky.
That's what this book is for!

Take the filling and wrappers out of the fridge and
begin to make dumplings! As soon as you have a
pan's worth, start cooking them up.

That's right, let's turn dumpling-
making into games! As a kid, I used
to challenge my friends to these fun
games. See if your guests are up for
it. If they are, here are three easy
competitions:

1. How many folds can you do
   on one dumpling?
2. How fast can you wrap a dumpling?
3. Who can make the most unique
   dumpling shape?
4. How many can you eat?

Winner gets dibs on hot dumplings!
*HAVE FUN!*

# CHAPTER 6

# DRINKS

Many of these drinks were inspired by the coolers I enjoyed growing up and also by the drinks served throughout China. Others I came up with when I craved something refreshing while taste-testing dumplings. All are perfect for pairing with Asian flavors. Of course, I've also created some tasty boozy drinks that are total winners among my friends. Whoever you're serving at the bar, you'll definitely have great options here.

# MINTY SUN TEA

During the holidays, John and I hoard the Candy Cane Minty Tea from Trader Joe's. It's so minty! I want to make sure I have enough to last me a year because I crave that intense mint flavor throughout the spring, summer, and fall.

6 fresh mint sprigs, plus
  more for garnish
6 bags mint tea or 6
  tablespoons (11 g) loose-
  leaf mint tea leaves

1  In a large pitcher, muddle the mint leaves. Add the tea and 2 quarts (2 L) room-temperature water. Stir well, then cover and let stand outside or by a window in the sun all day.

2  Strain the tea through a fine-mesh sieve, cover, and refrigerate until cold. Serve over ice and garnish with fresh mint.

Swap green tea leaves for the mint tea leaves to make iced green tea. But keep in the fresh mint leaves regardless. That makes it extra yummy.

Mix the tea with Ginger Limeade (page 182) for an Asian Arnold Palmer.

# THAI ICED COFFEE

MAKES ABOUT 2 QUARTS (2 L)

To re-create the same tall drink you enjoy in your favorite Thai restaurant, you need to buy powdered Thai coffee. It's called *oliang* and can be found online or in Thai markets. Once you've done that, the rest is easy.

6½ ounces (185 g) powdered
  Thai coffee
1 (12-ounce/340-g) can
  sweetened condensed milk

1  In a small saucepan, bring 2 quarts (2 L) water to a boil. Remove from the heat and stir in the coffee until dissolved. Let steep for 5 minutes.

2  Strain the coffee through a fine-mesh sieve lined with a clean kitchen towel or coffee filter. Stir in the sweetened condensed milk until well-mixed. Cover and refrigerate until very cold.

3  Stir once more and serve over ice.

I've always thought this classic Thai drink tastes like melted coffee ice cream. Yum.

# WATERMELON JUICE

MAKES ABOUT 2 QUARTS (2 L)

There's only one ingredient in this recipe, and that's a good thing. To get the most intense watermelon flavor, you want only watermelon. No simple syrup, no lemon juice, no bubbly water, and definitely no plain water. For the sweetest possible option, don't cut the watermelon too close to the rind. The good stuff's in the center.

10 cups (1.6 kg) chopped
   seedless watermelon (from
   about ½ melon), chilled

Place the watermelon in a blender or food processor and puree until very smooth. Divide among serving cups and serve immediately.

# CALAMANSI-ADE

MAKES ABOUT 2 QUARTS (2 L)

Calamansi is a citrus fruit from Southeast Asia that tastes like a tangerine and Meyer lemon got in a wrestling match. You're the winner! It's so tasty, you have to try it. You can't buy the fruits fresh here, but the concentrate is sold online and in Asian markets. It makes for a unique, sweet-tart cooler.

¾ cup (180 ml) calamansi
   juice concentrate
Pinch salt

In a large pitcher, stir the calamansi juice concentrate, salt, and 2 quarts (2 L) cold water until well-mixed. If necessary, refrigerate until cold. Serve over ice.

A shot of citrus vodka makes
this a pretty awesome hard
citrus-ade.

GINGER
SYRUP
(PAGE 183)

HONEYED
GINGER ALE
(PAGE 183)

PINEAPPLE
DRINKING
VINEGAR
(PAGE 182)

WATERMELON
JUICE

These
drinks are
thirsty
for you!

# GINGER LIMEADE

MAKES ABOUT 2 QUARTS (2 L)

A sip of this tangy refresher will make you feel as if you're sitting on grandma's porch. That is, if grandma was an awesome Thai chef.

2 cups (480 ml) fresh lime juice
2 cups (480 ml) Ginger Syrup (see opposite page)
¼ teaspoon kosher salt

In a large pitcher, combine the lime juice, Ginger Syrup, salt, and 1 quart (960 ml) cold water. Stir well. If necessary, refrigerate until chilled. Serve the limeade over ice.

Swap bubbly water for the regular water if you want to make a spritzer instead!

This is great to mix with a shot of gin or rum. Whoa! Fresh and rowdy all-in-one drink!

# PINEAPPLE DRINKING VINEGAR

MAKES ABOUT 2 QUARTS (2 L)

Drinking vinegar, sometimes called a switchel or shrub, is basically fruit vinegar for drinking. It's sour and sweet and very refreshing on hot days. This tropical version will get your appetite going for dumplings.

1 cup (240 ml) apple cider vinegar
⅔ cup (135 g) sugar
1 cup (165 g) diced ripe pineapple
2 quarts (2 L) soda water

1  In a large glass jar with a lid, stir together the vinegar and sugar to dissolve the sugar. Stir in the pineapple. Seal the jar and let sit at room temperature at least overnight and up to 4 days.

2  Strain through a fine-mesh sieve; discard the pineapple. Cover and refrigerate until cold.

3  Divide the mixture among eight glasses. Fill with ice, then top off with the soda water. Serve immediately.

# HONEYED GINGER ALE

MAKES ABOUT 2 QUARTS (2 L)

Whenever I was sick as a kid, my mom made me a hot concoction of honey and ginger. It was totally soothing. This is my take on that drink. I love the bubbly coolness of the soda water with the sharp kick of the ginger.

½ cup (120 ml) Ginger Syrup (see below)
2 quarts (2 L) soda water

Divide the syrup among eight glasses. Fill with ice, then top off with the soda water. Serve immediately.

## GINGER SYRUP

MAKES ABOUT 2 CUPS (480 ML)

Keep a jar of this simple syrup in the fridge and you'll always be ready to throw together a great drink. Of course, it's awesome in cocktails. A simple stir into hot water makes it a cure-all tonic, and topping it off with seltzer water means instant homemade soda.

1 cup (340 g) honey
¾ cup (75 g) sliced peeled fresh ginger
¼ teaspoon kosher salt

1   In a small saucepan, bring the honey, ginger, salt, and 1 cup (240 ml) water to a boil over high heat, stirring occasionally. Boil for 30 seconds, then cover and remove the pan from the heat. Let steep until the syrup is at room temperature, at least 20 minutes.

2   Strain through a sieve, pressing on the ginger to extract as much liquid as possible. Discard the ginger. The syrup can be refrigerated in an airtight container for up to 1 week.

Build on the soda base by adding ¼ teaspoon chili powder or ¼ cup (6 g) thinly sliced fresh Thai basil to the ginger syrup before simmering it.

# MICHELADAS

This would be my desert island drink. You know how people have a sweet tooth? I have a savory tooth, and this drink hits that tooth in all the right ways. The only thing better than cold beer with dumplings is a Michelada with dumplings. A Michelada is basically gussied-up beer. It is believed the name comes from the Spanish: *mi chela helada,* meaning "my cold beer." After trying it, you'll want this to be your cold beer.

Juice of 6 limes, plus wedges
    for serving
3 tablespoons mushroom soy
    sauce or liquid aminos
1 tablespoon Lawry's
    seasoning salt
1½ teaspoons kosher salt
6 heavy-handed shakes Tabasco
    sauce
6 (12-ounce/340-g) bottles
    Negro Modelo beer, chilled

1   In a pitcher, stir together the lime juice, soy sauce or liquid aminos, seasoning salt, kosher salt, and Tabasco. Open the beers and pour into the pitcher.

2   Fill six glasses with crushed ice and divide the Michelada among them. Serve immediately with lime wedges.

---

You can also set up a bar for guests to make their own Micheladas. Instruct them to take a swig or two of beer, then squeeze in the juice of a lime and add ½ teaspoon Lawry's, ¼ teaspoon salt, 1 ½ teaspoons soy sauce, and a shake of Tabasco. Have them hold a thumb over the bottle opening to keep it closed, then give the beer a gentle shake or two.

---

# SANGRIA

**I like serving sangria at parties because it feels so celebratory. Also because each drink comes with alcohol-soaked fruit that you can eat!**

1 lemon
2 large oranges
4 whole star anise
2 whole cloves
¼ cup (50 g) sugar
2 tablespoons Cointreau
1 (750-ml) bottle Pinot
  Grigio, chilled

1  Cut the lemon and 1 orange into quarters, then cut into thin slices. Transfer to a pitcher and squeeze in the juice of the other orange. Add the star anise, cloves, and sugar. Muddle the citrus with a wooden spoon. Cover the pitcher with plastic wrap and refrigerate for at least 2 hours or up to overnight.

2  Stir in the Cointreau and Pinot Grigio. Serve the sangria cold, ladling out chunks of fruit with the liquid. Mind the cloves and star anise as you drink!

Use a combo of regular
and blood oranges for
a mix of colors.

CHAPTER 7

DESSERTS

Ice cream is my dessert of choice. I always have at least a few cartons in the freezer. Some are my favorite supermarket brands, others I order specially from artisanal ice cream makers across the country. Whenever I'm craving something sweet, I grab a spoon and go at it.

For dumpling parties, though, I like to make special sweets. I usually keep it simple with homemade ice pops and slice-and-bake cookies, but sometimes I'll do a batch of chocolate soup dumplings. In the spirit of dumplings— and easy entertaining—I do only make-ahead desserts that are already in individual portions. They're more fun to eat that way and leave me free to hang out with my friends.

# CHOCOLATE SOUP DUMPLINGS

*New York Magazine* voted this one of the Top Ten Best Chocolate Desserts!

Be careful when you bite into this! The center's so melty, you might end up with chocolate all over your shirt.

MAKES 40 DUMPLINGS

Insane. These are just insane. You go from crackly, nutty black sesame shell to chewy sweet rice wrapper to silken chocolate "soup" center. Yeah, they're sort of a project, but I wouldn't have put them in this book if they weren't totally worth it. Trust me, they are.

**FOR THE FILLING:**
1½ pounds (680 g) high-quality semisweet chocolate, such as Callebaut, chopped
1 pound (455 g) unsalted butter
5 tablespoons (75 ml) brewed coffee

**FOR THE WRAPPERS:**
1 (1-pound/455-g) box Mochiko sweet rice flour
½ cup (100 g) sugar
2 ounces (55 g) wheat starch (see Note)
1½ teaspoons salt
2 tablespoons unsalted butter, softened
2 cups (480 ml) boiling water, plus more if needed
8 ounces (225 g) black sesame seeds
1 quart (960 ml) canola oil, plus more as needed

1  **Make the filling:** In a double-boiler or heatproof bowl set over a saucepan of simmering water, combine the chocolate and butter. Melt, stirring occasionally, until smooth. Whisk in the coffee until smooth. Remove the bowl from the heat and let cool to room temperature. Refrigerate until just firm.

2  Use the large side of a melon baller or a teaspoon measure or small cookie scoop to form the chocolate mixture into 40 small balls. Place the balls on a waxed paper–lined baking sheet, spacing them ½ inch (12 mm) apart. Refrigerate until firm. The balls can be refrigerated, very tightly wrapped with plastic wrap, for up to 2 weeks.

3  **Make the wrappers:** In the bowl of an electric mixer fitted with the paddle attachment, mix the rice flour, sugar, wheat starch, and salt on low speed until blended. With the machine running, add the butter and boiling water. Continue mixing until the dough is smooth, about 15 minutes. Add more water if the dough is too dry to come together.

4  Divide the dough into 40 equal portions. Dampen your hands and roll each piece of dough into a ball, rewetting your hands as needed to prevent the dough from sticking. Dampen your hands

again and flatten a ball into a thick disk. Place a ball of filling in the center and gather up the sides of the dough to encase the chocolate completely, pinching the seams to seal. Roll again to form a ball, then roll the dumpling in the black sesame seeds to evenly coat. Transfer to a wax paper–lined tray. Repeat with the remaining dough, chocolate, and sesame seeds.

5  Cover and refrigerate the dumplings until firm, at least 30 minutes or up to 3 days. You can also freeze them for up to 1 month.

6  In a large, heavy Dutch oven or saucepan, heat the oil over medium-high heat until hot but not smoking. If you drop a sesame seed in there, it should immediately sizzle but not burn. Add a few dumplings (don't crowd the pan!) and fry, turning occasionally, until crisp and slightly darkened, about 6 minutes. Adjust the heat as necessary to prevent them from cooking too quickly. Drain on paper towels. Repeat with the remaining dumplings. Serve hot or warm.

NOTE: Wheat starch isn't the same thing as wheat flour. I tried to substitute regular flour for it, and it really doesn't work. You can find wheat starch in Asian markets or specialty baking stores.

# MANGO LASSI ICE POPS

MAKES 1 DOZEN POPS

When it's super hot and humid out, I just want to pop one of these pops. Inspired by the cooling Indian drink, they've got a great balance of creaminess and spice.

2 cups (480 ml) plain whole-milk yogurt
2 cups (330 g) ripe mango chunks
1 cup (240 ml) mango juice
¼ cup (50 g) sugar
2 teaspoons freshly ground cardamom

1   In a blender, combine the yogurt, mango, mango juice, sugar, and cardamom. Puree until very smooth.

2   Divide among twelve 3-ounce (90-ml) pop molds. Insert sticks and freeze until very firm.

For an extra-special finishing touch, squeeze lime juice on the pop just before you serve it, and sprinkle it with a pinch of cayenne pepper and kosher salt.

# WATERMELON ICE POPS

MAKES 1 DOZEN POPS

These watermelon pops remind me of swimming pools. Growing up in L.A., I spent hot summer days by the pool, eating watermelon and letting the juices run all over my arms. I'd get so sticky, I'd hop in the pool to rinse off!

5 cups (775 g) chopped seedless watermelon
2 tablespoons fresh lime juice
2 tablespoons honey
1 teaspoon kosher salt

1   Place the watermelon in a blender or food processor and puree until very smooth. Press through a fine-mesh sieve and stir in the lime juice, honey, and salt.

2   Divide the mixture among twelve 3-ounce (90-ml) pop molds. Insert sticks and freeze until very firm.

MANGO
LASSI
ICE POPS

WATERMELON
ICE POPS

VIETNAMESE
COFFEE PUDDING
POPS
(PAGE 194)

# VIETNAMESE COFFEE PUDDING POPS

MAKES 15 POPS

Imagine coffee ice cream on a stick. But better. That's just what these pops are. They're like the fudgy pops you had as a kid, but with a deep richness from bittersweet chocolate and espresso. And the almond coating on the outside adds a killer crunch.

1 teaspoon unflavored powdered gelatin
1 cup (240 ml) heavy cream

½ cup (120 ml) sweetened condensed milk
1 tablespoon unsalted butter
1 ounce (30 g) bittersweet chocolate

⅛ teaspoon salt
¼ cup (60 ml) brewed espresso
1 cup (100 g) finely chopped roasted salted almonds

1 In a small bowl, sprinkle the gelatin over the cream and stir. Let soften for 5 minutes.

2 Meanwhile, in a heavy saucepan, combine the sweetened condensed milk, butter, chocolate, and salt. Heat over low heat, whisking occasionally, until melted and smooth. Whisk in the espresso, then the gelatin-cream mixture. Heat until steam rises off the top but before the mixture bubbles. Remove the pan from the heat.

3 Pour the mixture into fifteen 1-ounce (30-ml) cavities in silicone ice cube trays. Press a piece of plastic wrap directly against the surface. Freeze until firm.

4 Remove the ice cube tray from the freezer and let sit at room temperature for 10 minutes. Pop out the cubes. They should be moist and slightly soft. Place the almonds on a plate and roll the pops in the almonds to coat. Insert a stick in each pop and freeze again until firm.

The almond coating makes these super cute, like little dumplings on a stick. They're the perfect ending to a dumpling party!

# CARDAMOM RICE PUDDING

MAKES 8 SERVINGS

I like a little bite in my rice pudding. (Mushy stuff is for babies!) The basmati rice brings a touch of crunch—as does a final pistachio sprinkle—and a heady aroma, which cardamom elevates even further. I lightly sweeten the pudding itself to leave room for my tangy, sugary date chutney. If you're only making the pudding, you can add more sugar to taste.

**FOR THE DATE CHUTNEY:**
2 tablespoons unsalted butter
1½ cups (220 g) pitted dates,
   thinly sliced lengthwise
1 cup (240 ml) tamarind
   concentrate
¼ cup (55 g) packed brown
   sugar

1 teaspoon ground cumin
1 teaspoon ground red chile
½ teaspoon ground ginger

**FOR THE RICE PUDDING:**
1 cup (175 g) cooked basmati
   rice
1 cup (240 ml) whole milk

½ cup (120 ml) heavy cream
¾ cup (180 ml) coconut milk
¼ cup (50 g) granulated sugar
1 teaspoon ground cardamom
⅔ cup (80 g) shelled
   pistachios, toasted and
   coarsely chopped, for
   serving

1  **Make the date chutney:** In a medium saucepan, melt the butter over medium-high heat. Add the dates, tamarind, brown sugar, cumin, chile, ginger, and 1 cup (240 ml) water. Stir well and bring to a boil. Continue boiling, stirring frequently, for 10 minutes. Reduce the heat to low and simmer, stirring occasionally, until the chutney is nice and thick, about 15 minutes. Remove from the heat and let cool.

2  **Make the pudding:** In a large saucepan, bring the rice and milk to a boil. Reduce the heat to medium-low and simmer for 8 minutes. Stir in the cream, coconut milk, granulated sugar, and cardamom. Bring to a simmer, stirring occasionally.

3  Divide the pudding among serving bowls and top with the chutney and pistachios.

Whenever I serve this, my guests go from *oohs* and *aahs* to total silence while they dig in.

*ooh!*

*AAH!*

# MATCHA SHORTCUT SHORTBREAD

MAKES ABOUT 4 DOZEN COOKIES

This is a super easy cookie that you can make ahead for parties or to give as goodies. Matcha green tea powder can be found in tea shops and Japanese markets. That one ingredient makes these cookies green! Toasty! Melty! Salty! Sweet!

1 cup (225 g) unsalted butter, at room temperature

½ cup (100 g) sugar

Generous ¼ teaspoon kosher salt

2 tablespoons matcha green tea powder

1 teaspoon pure vanilla extract

2 cups (285 g) all-purpose flour

1 In a food processor, combine the butter, sugar, and salt. Process until fluffy, scraping down the bowl occasionally, about 3 minutes. Add the matcha and vanilla and process until evenly incorporated, scraping the bowl once or twice. Add the flour and pulse just until incorporated, scraping the bowl occasionally.

2 Transfer the dough to a piece of plastic wrap, forming it into a 12-inch- (30.5-cm-) long log. Wrap the plastic wrap around it and roll it to smooth out the sides. I like to press the log into a triangle shape, but you can keep it round or do another shape if you'd like. Refrigerate until firm, at least 1 hour and up to 1 day.

3 Preheat the oven to 325°F (165°C). Line cookie sheets with parchment paper.

4 Unwrap the dough and cut it into ¼-inch- (6-mm-) thick slices. Place the slices on the prepared sheets, spacing them 1 inch (2.5 cm) apart. Bake, rotating the positions of the pans halfway through, until the cookies are nicely browned around the edges, 12 to 15 minutes.

5 Cool completely on the pans on a wire rack. The shortbread can be stored in an airtight container at room temperature for up to 2 weeks.

Remember:
THE BETTER THE BUTTER,
THE BETTER THE BATTER!

# GREEN TEA–MARSHMALLOW TREATS

MAKES 12 SQUARES

This is so simple, I debated whether it was worth including in this book. But then I whipped up a batch, licked the melty green tea–infused marshmallow off the wooden spoon, and decided I had to put this one in. That smoky green tea savoriness that cuts through sweet marshmallows is rivaled only by its crazy green color. Perfect for the ultimate retro treat.

3 tablespoon unsalted butter, plus more for the dish

2 tablespoons matcha green tea powder
6 cups (275 g) mini marsh-mallows

⅛ teaspoon salt
6 cups (174 g) crisped rice cereal

1  Butter a 9-by-13-inch (23-by-33-cm) glass baking dish.

2  In a large skillet, melt the butter over medium-low heat. Add the matcha and whisk until smooth. Add the marshmallows and salt and gently stir with a wooden spatula until melted. Take your time; let the marshmallows melt slowly.

3  Add the cereal in thirds, gently stirring to evenly incorporate. Try not to crush the cereal too much! Remove from the heat and immediately transfer to the prepared pan. Press the mixture into an even layer, using a piece of waxed paper if you don't want to get your fingers sticky.

4  Let the treats cool completely in the pan, then cut into 12 squares. The treats can be stored in an airtight container at room temperature for up to 3 days.

# ACKNOWLEDGMENTS

**Kenny Lao**

This book has always belonged to the collective team. Speaking of teams, what an awesome team!

My editor at Abrams, Camaren Subhiyah, has really gotten behind my voice and style, even when I was trying to find both while working on this book. Throughout the intensive publishing process, Camaren was able to make me feel knowledgeable and taken care of.

My agent, Kari Stuart at ICM, always has my back (and the rest of me as well!).

The look and feel of the book can be accredited to Sebit Min. She is by far the coolest person on this team and also lives the farthest out on the L train. I am so psyched that she worked with us on this book and that I can count myself as one of the lucky authors to have her attention and eye.

Lucy Schaeffer shot the first batch of dumplings created by chef Anita Lo for Rickshaw back in 2004. She was a photo editor at *Food & Wine* wanting to build her own portfolio, and I was a new restaurant owner. She did that first shoot and many others for cost, with chef Anita or me as the only stylist. Since then she has gone on to photograph more than forty cookbooks, and it was amazing to see her on set with a crew of more than fifteen people for this shoot. I saw her and said, "This is a long cry from my holding a light reflector for you on Barrow Street!"

I would have never undertaken this book project had it not been for my coauthor, Genevieve Ko. She understood my voice, what I was trying to say when I couldn't say it, what flavors I was trying to make when I couldn't make them, and what direction I should go in when I was at a fork (or spoon) in the road. It was a gift to be able to spend time with her in the kitchen and to see her endless approaches to the efficiency tangent. She is creative, thoughtful, technical, and precise with a dream. She rocks.

And without a doubt the biggest acknowledgment goes to the spouse. Without John, there would be no sweet potato dumpling, and I cannot imagine the world without one.

Go team!

## Genevieve Ko

Many thanks to Kenny for bringing so much energy and enthusiasm to this project. And for bringing Zipper to our testing sessions to keep my kitchen floors clean and my kids happy. This book wouldn't have happened if Virginia and Mateo Jaramillo hadn't introduced us years ago. Thanks for hosting that Brooklyn brunch and being such great food friends.

The whole team at Stewart, Tabori & Chang has turned a simple dumpling idea into a great book. Thanks to Leslie Stoker for acquiring it, Holly Dolce for getting us going, and Camaren Subhiyah for seeing us through to the end, and thanks to managing editor Sally Knapp and production manager True Sims. Lucy Schaeffer's photography is stunning, as is Sebit Min's design. Thanks also to our agents, Kari Stuart and Angela Miller.

I'm grateful, as always, for my family. Thanks for your love, support, and endless enthusiasm for eating dumplings.

# INDEX

Published in 2015 by Stewart, Tabori & Chang
An imprint of ABRAMS

Library of Congress Control Number: 2014959139
ISBN: 978-1-61769-156-0

Editor: Camaren Subhiyah
Designer: Sebit Min
Production Manager: True Sims

The text of this book was composed in Century Gothic,
Apercu Pro, and Prestige Elite.

Printed and bound in the United States

10 9 8 7 6 5 4 3 2 1

Stewart, Tabori & Chang books are available at special
discounts when purchased in quantity for premiums and
promotions as well as fundraising or educational use.
Special editions can also be created to specification.
For details, contact specialsales@abramsbooks.com or the
address below.

ABRAMS
THE ART OF BOOKS SINCE 1949

115 West 18th Street
New York, NY 10011
www.abramsbooks.com